The
Great Hurricane:
1938

The
Great Hurricane:
1938

CHERIE BURNS

Atlantic Monthly Press
New York

Published simultaneously in Canada
Printed in the United States of America

Library of Congress Cataloging-in-Publication Data
Burns, Cherie.
    The great hurricane—1938 / Cherie Burns.
        p. cm.
    Includes bibliographical references and index.
    ISBN 0-87113-893-X
    1. Hurricanes—New York (State)—Long Island—History—20th century.   2. Long Island (N.Y.)—History—20th century.   3. Long Island (N.Y.)—Biography.   I. Title.
    F127.L8B93 2005
    974.7'21043—dc22   2005041211

Atlantic Monthly Press
an imprint of Grove/Atlantic, Inc.
841 Broadway
New York, NY 10003

05 06 07 08 09   10 9 8 7 6 5 4 3

for Dick, Alex, and Jessie

Confronting a storm is like fighting God. All the powers in the universe seem to be against you and in an extraordinary way, your irrelevance is at the same time both humbling and exalting.

—Frances Legrande

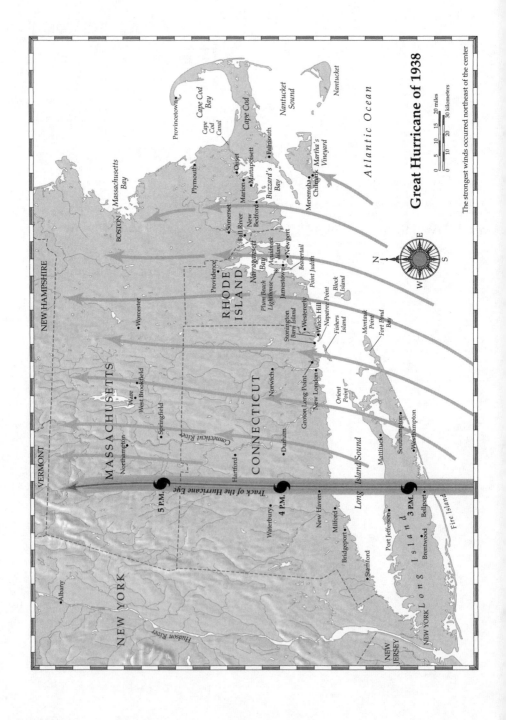

Great Hurricane of 1938

The strongest winds occurred northeast of the center

Introduction

I first heard about the Great Hurricane of 1938 from a friend in Nantucket. She explained that her mother felt anxious when visiting her seaside cottage during rainy weather or when she felt the rhythm of the waves rising through the floorboards on certain summer nights. Her grandmother had been killed in a hurricane in Rhode Island that had swept hundreds of people off the beach, she said. I had never heard of such a thing, especially in New England. I had seen newscasts of the victims of hurricanes in Florida and the Caribbean, but their losses were mainly property since they had always been evacuated well ahead of time.

A few years later I heard again of the Great Hurricane of 1938. I was with a woman from Rhode Island who mentioned that her grandparents had both drowned in "the big hurricane in Rhode Island." By then I had seen for myself what a hurricane can do. I was in Nantucket in August 1991 when Hurricane Bob hit the East Coast. I got a firsthand look at the damage I had seen before only on television. No lives were lost in Nantucket that year, but fallen trees made the streets of our village impassable. Power and water were knocked out for several days, and in its wake was a bitter parching of all the summer foliage. The 110-mile-per-hour winds and salt spray stripped all the trees or turned them brown overnight. Summer ended in a day. Some deciduous trees never recovered. As I drove into Nantucket town the morning after, I saw the masts of sailboats in the harbor tilted at a sickening 45 degrees. Another boat had been driven into a restaurant. The clear sky and winking bright sun sparkled in the moisture still trapped in the air, like a sly wink after some act of treachery. It took weeks to clean and repair the damage.

That same fall another storm came to Nantucket. The October 11 storm, which would become known as the infamous "perfect storm," wreaked much more damage on both Long Island and Nantucket. The local Nantucket newspaper made a video I watched later on Thanksgiving. No footage had ever affected me as did that black-and-white tape of two middle-aged sisters hurrying to remove what they could from their seaside house, just down the bluff from ours, before the waves claimed it. Then came the worst. In an eerily silent scene, the house rode slowly out to sea on the waves. For several moments it swayed and drifted like a houseboat, and then the vertical white trim along the roof and sides collapsed like Popsicle sticks. A final surge of waves with whitecapped spray rose and the house was gone, swallowed whole by the sea.

Soon after, I read about the Great Hurricane of 1938 in *The Perfect Storm*. In making his point that a mature hurricane is the most powerful event on earth, author Sebastian Junger mentioned that in the Hurricane of 1938, the waves shook the earth so hard that they were registered by a seismograph five thousand miles away in Alaska. The "perfect storm" that swept away the crew of the *Andrea Gail* in the Grand Banks of the Atlantic was of considerably lesser magnitude than the 1938 hurricane. The Great Hurricane of 1938 seems to have earned a little-known place in the annals of sea history despite its wider anonymity. When later I spoke with a friend, an excellent sailor, who talked about sailboat racing off the spit of sand that is now Napatree Point, I told him the point was once lined with gracious summer cottages and that children in woolen swimsuits played in the surf in front of the houses off Fort Road. I could see that he didn't believe me.

Why, I began to wonder, was this legendary hurricane not better known? Except for the above references, televised anniversary specials during hurricane season, and a few books compiled from newspaper accounts and historical collections, the Great Hurricane of 1938 had been largely forgotten. Yet everyone I asked who had lived through it knew about the tragedy. To them it was a milestone event like Kennedy's assassination, Pearl Harbor day, or even September 11. The answer lay partly in history. The day after the hurricane, Hitler's troops moved into Czechoslovakia and the news media were mesmerized by the emerging specter of World War II. As a result, the Great Hurricane came and ripped its way from Long Island to

Providence without the nation ever comprehending the enormity of the disaster.

Even when predicted, hurricanes are experiences no one forgets. I recently spent an evening with a woman from St. Thomas who tried to explain to me the sensation of pressure bearing down on her head that accompanied the hurricane she had experienced in the tropics in 1995. She talked of her roof buckling, of watching furniture blow out the door of her house, and of the shattering sound of breaking glass and splintering trees and furniture as clearly as if they'd happened yesterday. The hurricane winds sounded like the roar of a speeding freight train, she recalled. It was the same description I'd heard from the survivors of the Great Hurricane. This woman also spoke of the post-traumatic depression survivors experienced, and I made note that not one of the nearly fifty survivors I interviewed for this book spoke of depression or flagging mental health following the Great Hurricane of 1938.

In reporting this book, I have come to believe that, sixty-five years after a disaster, people have forgotten the emotional trauma that came in its wake. They focus instead on the drama of the event, and it is the active elements of the disaster that fascinated them then and now. That's what seems to lodge in memory. Back then people didn't talk a lot about how they *felt*, perhaps because they didn't have the luxury of doing so with the Depression at their backs and the outbreak of another world war ahead. In 1938 people seemed to get on with life, no matter how dismal the prospect.

I was also amazed at the way memory plays tricks with people in extreme circumstances. The experience of a disaster is clearly so intense that it seems to bend the laws of physics and make people believe they witnessed impossible events. I heard of a car being picked up by the wind and hurled into a pond like a toy and of a little boy blown up into the air like someone in a Harry Potter story until his nanny, in the nick of time, grabbed him by the foot and yanked him back to earth. The ferocious experience of the hurricane was so far outside the normal boundaries of routine occurences that many people believe things happened that clearly didn't, or were exaggerations of the real events.

What is it about a disaster that captivates our imagination? Is it the thrill of the unexpected, the kick of vicarious adrenaline we get wondering what we would have done under such uncontrollable circumstances? I feel certain that I would not have handled herding my children onto the roof of a house in rising water and being blown into the unknown as coolly as Catherine Moore reportedly did. I lose my cool when there is a leak on the front porch, so how would I cope with the devastation and debris that the hurricane made of many people's homes? I guess that's the point. Each account of people who survived the disaster of the Great Hurricane of 1938 becomes a facet of understanding the way people respond and survive that we can imagine and measure ourselves against. *What would I have done?* in the same situation, we ask, and the provocation of the question illustrates why we like to read about disasters that befall other people. In learning about the story of a real disaster, there is a craving for more than the vicarious kick. As we sit alone, safely warm and dry at home in armchairs reading about the 100-mile-per-hour winds and rising water, it puts us to the test.

I asked myself when I first heard about the Great Hurricane of 1938, how could a hurricane have hit while people were picnicking and playing on the beach? Didn't they pay attention to the warnings? Weren't there signs in the weather that even laymen would recognize? As I delved into this story, I learned how far forecasting the weather has come in sixty-five years. Our landscaper came to spread fertilizer on our lawn in Nantucket last week on a perfectly sunny morning without a cloud in the sky because he knew it would rain that night. In 1938 such a sure prediction was unheard-of. Forecasting the weather was a primitive art, and communications to reach the public were severely limited. We can hardly imagine a time when the public didn't know what was coming its way.

The Great Hurricane of 1938 was the strongest and most destructive storm ever to hit New England, and one of the most powerful natural events in recorded history. It was an unrivaled disaster from which some communities would never recover physically, economically, or spiritually. Flowing through the account of the hurricane's quick, brutal passage are the personal stories of the people who experienced its rage in their coastal communities. This book is the story of these events and the people who experienced them, of how on a mostly clear September day, seven hundred people lost their lives when the Great Hurricane took them by surprise.

I

Milt Miller was awake by five. Like the whalers and fishermen in his family before him, he'd always been an early riser. He'd started fishing, he liked to say around Montauk, as soon as he could walk. Now that fishing was good, he often stayed on board the boat overnight to make the most of each day. His wife of three years was used to that, and he was making over two hundred dollars a month, which made it easier. When he came up on deck of the 110-foot dragger, the dawn sky was hazy but unremarkable. The sea was flat calm. There had been stars in a clear sky the night before when he turned in after he and the rest of the five-man crew had iced and shipped a boatload of cod and porgies west to New York City. Fish was bringing in ten cents a pound. Life, for a twenty-five-year-old man conditioned by the Depression, was pretty good. But as he moved slowly into the day, preparing to take the boat out and pick up a net they'd left the night before on Gardiners Island, an eighty-year-old fisherman on the dock called out, "If you're going to go, you'd better get over there and get back. I've never seen the barometer so low." Milt took note. He knew the old-timer had what fishermen called a "weather eye," a squint that could tell what the weather was going to be better than any other kind of forecast.

Montauk Point, at the end of Long Island, thrusts east toward the dawn while the rest of America is still in darkness. To the northwest lay Long Island Sound, and just over the horizon were the sleeping coasts of Connecticut and Rhode Island. East toward the sun was the Atlantic. Tidal waters swirled around the point, into the sound, and back again, carrying schools of bait and the larger fish that fed on it. There was money to be pulled from the gray waters off Montauk.

Milt pulled away from the dock at the Promised Land fish factory and eased the boat across mirror-flat waters toward the sound. It had been nearly 2:00 A.M. when he finally moored the boat and went to sleep the night before, but he was a vigorous, chunky young man and could get by on a few hours' sleep when the fishing was good. He loved to fish.

When the fishing boats set out to sea at the start of the day, Milt felt exhilarated. He watched the *Ocean View*, a bunker steamer that belonged to the Smith Meal Company, the biggest fish factory in Montauk, set out with the other boats. Its crew fished for menhaden, the small, bony fish used in making soap and fertilizer.

Also heading out the harbor, going toward the point, was a trawler from Fort Pond Bay dock. He knew it was

Capt. Dan Grimshaw's boat and that his friend, Stevie Dellapolla, was on board. Dellapolla, eighteen, was busily squaring away the deck, but he waved when he saw Milt. He felt good when he saw Milt Miller. Everyone knew Milt, who had been fishing since his early teens, longer than any of the other young men. Stevie also much admired his brother-in-law, Andrew Samb, a fisherman who had gone out on a bunker boat, the *Robert E.*, that morning. Stevie was proud to be working as a fisherman.

Dan Grimshaw was known as an able captain. Navigational equipment was minimal and consisted of a compass, a radio, and a direction finder only, so the captain's skill and knowledge of weather and sea conditions and handling the boat were every bit as important as the vessel's seaworthiness. Stevie felt in good hands with him. He had spent a lot of time on the boat that fall, because its trips alternated between commercial dragging and party-fishing, and so far they had been party-fishing three days a week when the passenger train brought out clients.

Often, when the train didn't bring anyone, they went swordfishing. That was a very specialized technique. First, a crewman standing in the bow would harpoon the swordfish, which had a habit of basking on the surface. Then two men would pick up a small barrel on the bow and throw it overboard. Inside the barrel was six hundred feet of line tied to the harpoon. When the fish took off, the barrel bobbed along behind and marked where the fish was going. It was a smaller version of a similar method used for whaling in these waters a hundred years before. Stevie was learning a lot, and also earning $2.50 a trip. On this morning, as Milt's

boat moved away toward the northwest and Gardiners Island, Stevie noticed that Dan Grimshaw was staring intently
at the horizon.

Grimshaw had noticed the sudden drop in the barometer that signals the approach of high winds and bad
weather. Like a giant vacuum cleaner, the low pressure in
the eye of the storm was already drawing the air south. He
listened to the radio, but there was no advisory. Halfway
out to the fishing grounds, when the barometer neared 29
inches, he turned back. He wanted to reach a good mooring before whatever was coming hit. After they'd turned,
Stevie watched the forty-foot lobster boats go by, continuing out to the ocean. The crews were busy with the excitement in anticipation of a storm, and working to secure their
gear and lines. Still, a few of the men paused to wave at
Stevie. Stevie caught the eye of some of the crewmen. Later,
he thought he had seen a manic gleam in their eyes. He had
a sense of foreboding, and thought they did, too. Something
just told him, he said later, that they were waving good-bye.

II

That low barometer, none of the fishermen knew at the time, signaled the approach of a frighteningly powerful hurricane that was approaching them at the unheard-of speed of 67 miles per hour. Its center was surrounded by tightly wrapped winds reaching 156 miles per hour. It was pushing a storm surge ahead of it that would raise coastal water levels as much as forty feet. About two hundred miles across, it would sweep north across Long Island, then Long Island Sound, and then smash into the coasts of Connecticut and Rhode Island, devastating blue-blood resorts and blue-collar mill communities with equal vengeance.

This hurricane was to leave a lasting scar in the collective memory of the regions it struck. Its violence was far beyond the experience of the seaside dwellers it assaulted, and they were not prepared as we are all today by television clips showing such storms elsewhere. They could not imagine what it would be like, even had they been warned.

Newspapers and radio stations outside the immediate area, filled with international news, didn't report the storm very well. Media and communications within the storm area were hugely disrupted, so it was difficult for both individuals and the nation to grasp the totality of what had happened. A hurricane is less like one huge disaster than it is the sum of a thousand smaller tragedies. Once those tragedies were recorded, Long Islanders and New Englanders have always spoken of the event, long before hurricanes were named by the government, as the Great Hurricane of 1938.

GH38 hit the nation, and particularly the Northeast, at a vulnerable time. The region, tied as it was to industry and the economies of big cities, was beginning to regroup after the Depression. The fishermen of Long Island like Milt Miller felt life was good for them, but they also knew that people were going without food in New York City. Rich and poor, from the starchy Connecticut upper classes to the immigrant inhabitants of the yeastier neighborhoods of Providence, had downsized their lives and expectations after the market crash of '29.

Everyone skimped. A middle-class twelve-year-old boy could consider ten cents a respectable weekly allowance. In some states a woman couldn't teach once she married so as not to take a paying job away from a man who had a family to support. College and boarding school enrollments were down because of the hard times, and men and women both young and old worked in the textile mills and factories in Providence and Boston despite the lack of opportunity for advancement. Spinning, weaving, and the dyeing of cloth had been big business for the nation's garment industry, centered in Providence and Boston since the early 1800s. Yet now the streets were full of the poor, especially the thousands of immigrant Irish, Italian, and Portuguese millworkers who had been laid off first as the Northeastern textile industry lost supremacy to the South and then by the retrenchment of the Depression. Maiden aunts became spinsters who moved in to help others with their children and housework in return for room and board.

The Depression perhaps took its highest toll on the prospects and optimism of the young. New high school graduates were typically law-abiding and respected authority. Many of them had hardly known anything except economic hard times. The 25 percent unemployment rate was frightening enough, and people knew that any trouble with the police would make getting a job even more difficult. Still, six months after graduation, only one in four high school graduates was employed. Many pared down their ambitions to live on their own and often stayed home because it was affordable, and their contribution to the family's invariably strained household budget was sorely needed. Paying room and board to one's parents, even handing over one's paycheck to receive an allowance back, was a common practice.

Those lucky enough to have jobs in the cities worked in offices and shops downtown, rode the nickel trolley to work, and lived to go to the movies on weekends. In a world without shopping centers and cineplexes, cities were thriving centers of life and pinnacles of sophisticated urbanity. It was the age of the American department store like Cherry & Webb in Providence and B. Altman's in New York. Though often cavernous and poorly lit, they made shoppers feel that they were in the land of plenty, removed from the world of want out on the street, even if they could only afford to window-shop beneath often gaily striped, stately awnings. For everything from furniture to silk stockings, department stores were the places to shop, and they made shopping enjoyable with their luxurious ladies' lounges and furniture displays, sometimes even cafeterias or tearooms on the mezzanine. They were full of bustle and anonymous female salesclerks with flawless makeup and window displays showing just what to wear and how to decorate one's home. Everyone escaped the drudgery of daily life by going downtown.

It was considered almost un-American to not go to the movies once a week, and in a life pared down to economic necessities and daily duties, luxurious downtown theaters were as close to heaven as most people could get. It was the golden age of movies, and Hollywood projected a population's thwarted ambitions and frustrations during the Depression and filled their fantasies. A public burdened by the economic and psychological impact of eight hard years found relief—and escape—at the movies. Favorite films were light-hearted capers like *Bringing Up Father* and featured stars like Errol Flynn in *Captain Blood*. Bing Crosby, with his wholesome good looks and carefree singing voice, was a favorite, as were Laurel and Hardy. Joan Bennett, who customarily played a madcap heiress and wore fabulous gauzy, shimmering clothes with square shoulders and defined waists above fitted hips, was a favorite of women. Her riches and spirited frivolity as she jilted and reclaimed endless rich, handsome suitors on-screen fueled their fantasies of romantic escape from the hard-bitten realities of their off-screen lives.

Despite the hardships, progress and innovation continued, albeit slowly. In 1938, Du Pont first marketed a miracle fabric called nylon. Big prints and patterns were in vogue, and nylon encouraged designers to favor midcalf-length skirts that flowed as freely as silk but were more affordable. The first nylon toothbrush was marketed in New Jersey. The New York Yankees won their third consecutive world championship, and a chain letter craze challenged the postal service with a huge burden of extra mail. Women worked, but mostly in domestic and clerical positions, and an unmarried thirty-year-old was automatically declared a spinster. Almost never was a married woman referred to by her first name, even in the newspaper. And racial divides were equally clear. Blacks, called colored, had their own obituary section in the newspaper.

Bugs Bunny made his screen debut, but comic books and cartoon strips were the new rage that entered almost every house. Action comics were created, starring Captain Marvel and Superman and Sheena, Queen of the Jungle. Blondie, with her tart tongue and Dagwood's foibles, was the first comic strip that mocked and had a little fun with middle-class mores. The public was ready to look at itself and have a laugh. Life wasn't only about struggle, people hoped.

Radio was the medium that tapped the public consciousness and mattered to advertisers. It was all there was and, except for papers and weeklies, the public followed it for news and entertainment broadcasts. Some 75 percent of all homes had a radio set. Sunday nights most people stayed close to home to listen to *The Jack Benny Program*. The radio audience was so large that when H. G. Wells's *War of the Worlds* was performed on *The Mercury Theatre on the Air* that same year, listeners mistook it for news that Martians had indeed landed, and a national panic followed until announcers could convince listeners that what they'd been listing to was only fiction. Ivory soap, Oxydol laundry detergent, and Crisco shortening were the leading advertisers and sponsors, and they knew that radio reached the audience they were looking for.

Still, a stunting in the American consciousness had already occurred. America, so indomitably spirited and optimistic on one hand, had learned undeniably about fear at home during the Depression. President Roosevelt's slogan that there was nothing to fear but fear itself allayed some of the anxieties, but such times would never be forgotten by those who lived through them. Now the news from abroad didn't look much better to those who read the papers, listened to the radio, or saw the most dramatic and compelling account of world affairs—in a world without television—in the Movietone newsreels.

The breadlines and soup kitchens were constant reminders that poverty was still licking at the nation's heels. Even debutantes were denied new gowns and often recycled the previous season's fashions. Dreams and college educations were deferred. Some of the unemployed joined federal works projects such as the WPA to make ends meet, and a developing welfare system and network of social workers championed by first lady Eleanor Roosevelt, who was photographed routinely in her cloth coat and clunky shoes, reaching out to the poor, put a lifeline out to the poorest. Eleanor was a favorite with the public, a rich first lady who eschewed the privileges of wealth.

The late 1930s were an otherwise quiet time in the United States, presided over by President Franklin Roosevelt, who tried to boost morale as much as the actual economy. As the nation emerged from its crouch, it romanticized the bedrock pioneer values of home, hearth, and living off the bounty of the land that some considered to be America's most authentic face, anyhow. In reality, rural life had already been overshadowed by the American industrial revolution and Wall Street wealth in the Northeast, but as belts were tightened everywhere, the virtues of simple living became fashionable. Even the rich denied themselves flashy finery and advertising that they were rich. It would have been unbecoming.

The razzle-dazzle of the Jazz Age and the Roaring Twenties had left their mark on the 1930s, but their glamour and profligacy seemed distant after nine years of Depression. There had been wild parties and new fashions, but underneath the bobbed haircuts, shimmies, and cigarette smoke, life stayed pretty much the same for most people. Newspapers on Long Island had gone so far as to interview some of the girls, the "flappers," who danced until dawn. The papers revealed that the girls hurried home in time to enter bread-baking contests the next morning.

For most people, that's how real life was, somewhere between the glitzy proclamation of changed manners and

morals and life as usual. Life had a way of coming back to
center, and the stock market crash of 1929 made certain that
everyone sobered up after the high times. Prohibition and
the rum-running boon of the early 1930s were over, though
they had shaped Long Island's and much of the Northeast's
coastal economies for a while, not always illegally. One boat-
yard in Freeport, Long Island, made thirty boats for rumrunners and fifteen for the Coast Guard to chase them in. But
by 1933, when Prohibition ended, the flash of money, the thrill
of living dangerously, and the high times were gone. Only the
faintest echo of Billie Holiday, Sophie Tucker, and other jazz
greats who had packed the roadhouses along the south shore
frequented by glamorous gangsters like Legs Diamond remained in some folks' memories. The opulence had been
supplanted by more somber realities for nearly everyone.
In the Northeast, the most severe contractions of the Depression continued.

By 1937 the stock market was showing signs of life
again and the well-to-do were starting to feel some finan-
cial relief, but the Depression psychology was harder to
shake. One twelve-year-old heir to his father's railroad fortune was told by his playmates on New York's Upper East
Side that he was rich. He was quite sure that he wasn't, the
way that money and the economy were discussed at home,
and the epithet made him uncomfortable during the hard
times. Everyone thought poor.

Wealthy New Englanders had long been partial to the
region's waterfront for their leisure activities. A scenic coastline lined with mile after mile of sand dunes and inlets had
become their playground as soon as automobiles and rail-

roads could provide the affluent with connections between the shore and their lives in the cities. Enchanting waterfront villages and yacht clubs had been built up from the Connecticut coast through Rhode Island and Massachusetts. Fathers and husbands could work in inland towns and come down to the shore on weekends during the sweltering heat of July and August while their families "summered" at the beach. It was an ideal that had taken root at the turn of the century.

In Long Island, boardinghouses in the mid-nineteenth century gave way to resort hotels, and by the 1930s a network of sportsmen, artists, bootleggers, and Wall Street titans had settled along the island's eighty-mile-long coast. Some were pleased to call it the Glittering Alley. The debutante parties, sprawling summerhouses, yachting parties, and entertainments were precursors to the modern, fashionable Hamptons.

But ironically, it was the Depression that helped develop that Yankee trait that had become the hallmark of class and breeding in the Northeast: restraint and lack of ostentation. As the rich went about oufitting their summerhouses, it seemed unseemly to be extravagant about it while thousands were selling pencils on the street and living in shantytowns. It was a matter of good taste. So New York and Rhode Island matrons did their houses in ginghams and wicker and extolled the virtues of simplicity. Summerhouses were places to relax without the need to keep up with the Joneses the way one did in Hartford, Boston, or New York. There was an unmistakable preciousness to the gentility, like the prosperous women who went to their summer homes and

gardened wearing pearls. Those were the days when banking magnate Otto Kahn in Southampton built one-hundred-
room mansions, but talked of the need for "atoning" for his
wealth with good works. There would always be millionaires
who lived large. Yet the style and character that became the
status symbols of the time, especially in the developing resort
communities, were modest and restrained in 1938, in a New
England kind of way.

It was the gentle coastline, especially along Long Island and the filigreed inlets of Connecticut and Rhode Island,
that distinguished the East Coast shorefront and attracted
devoted homeowners and vacationers. Sailors had long fa-
vored the network of cozy maritime communities and harbors that had become established by commercial fishermen
and explorers soon after the arrival of the Pilgrims. Unlike
the dramatic cliffs that plunge down to the surf along the
West Coast, miles of luxurious sand dunes stretched along
the beaches of the Atlantic and Long Island Sound. The
barrier beaches, an East Coast phenomenon created over
time when flooded backwater shifted the sandy ocean floor
to build a ribbon of beach, protected homeowners from high
tides and rough waves, and encouraged them to build houses
on these narrow strips of sand, with the ocean in front and
tidal ponds behind. They built as close to the water as they
could, sometimes leaving only a few hundred feet between
the front porch steps and the waves lapping at the waterline. In areas like Weekapaug and Napatree Point in Rhode
Island, it was possible to look out to sea from the living room
windows, and inland over the pond or bay from the back
porch or kitchen window of many houses. Yacht clubs, their

flags fluttering, and moorings for boats large and small
speckled the inlets and ponds. Bridges and causeways had
been built to provide automobile access across the barrier
ponds out to the houses along the beach. It was not unusual
to drive seven miles along the dune roads to reach a house
perched looking proudly out to sea, and nobody thought
twice about it. New Englanders as a whole were relatively
stalwart about the weather. To be undeterred by hard win-
ters or wind and rain was a point of pride. As in England,
mudrooms and entry halls outfitted with slickers, boots, and
rain hats were common testimony that the inhabitants were
not to be kept from their chores, sports, or other activities
by a little harsh weather.

In 1938, watching storms, especially at the time of the
equinox when tides were highest, was considered a pleasur-
able pastime. "Linestorms," as the locals called locally severe squalls that moved in a dark line across the waters more
frequently in the early fall, were nothing to worry about.
They provided a touch of drama to the changing seasons,
and couples thought these small storms were more romantic than dangerous. It was not uncommon to see young men
and women huddled together on the beach gazing out at the
swirling whitecaps, liberated by the excitement of the gusty
winds and the raindrops that pelted their faces. They did
not live as we do today in constant media-fed disaster awareness. Earthquakes in Tokyo and Turkey, great storms in the
Philippines, and hideous plane crashes weren't part of the
evening news. A train wreck made the news in the papers,
but it was a time of relative innocence from the grisly details
of disaster.

Contrary to certain hurricane lore that developed after the devastation of the hurricane, the tides that September were no higher than they had been during the equinox in previous years. Rather, it was the convergence of factors that made GH38 into such a disaster. The high winds and tidal surge arrived on their own schedule, coincidentally, during high tide. Inland rainfall and flooding had already swelled rivers and waterlogged the forests' floors, making trees and buildings more vulnerable than usual to high winds. In addition, GH38 became what meteorologists now know is an extratropical cyclone, one that intensifies and enlarges as its warm center decays, cools, and elongates, increasing its staying power even as it is losing strength. These factors were unlucky for the population, by chance.

In the fall of 1938, as in previous Septembers, home-owners from Springfield, Massachusetts, and Providence, Rhode Island, seized the chance to drive down to the shore to put up the shutters for winter and sneak in a final sail or day at the beach. Rain they expected, since the air was humid and oppressive when people went to bed all up and down the East Coast. For those who listened to the radio, the news was beginning to sound portentous. Neville Chamberlain was giving in to Hitler's demands in Europe, but at least those troubles were over there, across the ocean. Northeasterners felt safe at home, lulled by a gradually improving economy and President Roosevelt's sonorous reassurances to them on the evening radio. No one knew that a monster was headed their way. No one told them.

III

Huracán, in the language of the pre-Columbian Carib of the Caribbean, was the storm god. He was an evil and wildly unpredictable deity, as storms were in those days. Now, thanks to satellites, radar, hurricane-hunter planes, and a myriad of other high-tech devices, hurricanes are remarkably predictable. Hurricane Andrew, which ripped across the Bahamas, Florida, and Louisiana in 1992, traveled west across the Atlantic along the "hurricane alley" course that GH38 had taken fifty-four years before and was perhaps the single most destructive hurricane in U.S. history. Though Andrew carved a thousand-mile swath of devastation to property, only twenty people died. It had been tracked by satellite and radar for days. Its predicted arrival time and place were broadcast nonstop by radio and television, and the predictions were accurate. Nearly 1 million people were evacuated before the hurricane made landfall.[1]

The Great Hurricane of 1938 was in a different era. Its beginning was unremarkable; it seems to have been born about September 4 in the waters around the Cape Verde Islands, in the Doldrums roughly four hundred miles off the coast of Senegal, where most Atlantic hurricanes start. This mostly windless, somnolent region, which has plagued sailing captains since sea travel began with its mix of tedious calms and unexpected savage squalls, is a breeding ground for the tropical waves, or mild troughs of low pressure, that grow into hurricanes. Most such disturbances dissipate, but on average four tropical cyclones in the Atlantic whirl to tropical storm maturity every year—if all the other variables are right. The surface water temperature off Cape Verde is typically warm enough in late summer (81 degrees and above) to begin the tropical cyclone "system" that makes a hurricane.

One can only guess at the small disturbance, perhaps a gentle puff of hot air off the Sahara or some mild irregularity in the concentration of the sun's warmth on a patch of sea, that created a spot of warm air well enough defined to rise and pull in the slightly cooler air from below. The undulating line of the tropical wave of air around such a spot will sometimes twist. If it twists far enough, the system starts to curve and shape itself around a core. Eventually this small cell starts spinning so fast that no new air can get into the center, and the eye is formed. The warm air that fuels a hurricane rises up the whirling wall of wind. Skies must be clear enough so that the funnel of circulating air won't be capped at the top and collapse. Without satellite pictures and tracking planes, it is hard to know for certain, but GH38 most likely encountered or created cirrus clouds that diverged and circled out, allowing it to build and blow until its circulating speed had reached 10 to 12 knots. At this point, like a car with its engine revved and ready to go, all it needed was an open highway to travel. And that is what the pathway called "hurricane alley" provides in late summer, when the Atlantic guides hurricanes along a familiar route.

Weather patterns that carry a hurricane are a bit like a highway. The Bermuda High, a settled high-pressure area that swells and contracts seasonally, dominates wind patterns over the North Atlantic and determines the tracks of Atlantic hurricanes as they move west. In winter, when temperatures are low, the high is small; but July through September, when water temperatures are much warmer, it expands over the entire center of the North Atlantic. Its area of high pressure functions like a barrier wall that low-pressure tropical cyclones cannot penetrate. So they skirt west in the Atlantic along its southern flank and travel around its western edge to the Caribbean or the waters just north of it. Then, as they approach the coast of the United States, they begin to be influenced by the weather systems that move across the country and out to sea. They turn toward the north. Whether they will ease to the northwest, or curve north, or continue curling northeast until they are guided into the North Atlantic's cooler waters is the crucial question for hurricane forecasters.

It took GH38 seventeen days to make the journey. On the eighteenth of September, the storm was first reported and identified for what it was by the Brazilian merchant ship SS *Alegrete*, three hundred miles north of Puerto Rico. A day later it was in the Bahamas and appeared to be headed straight for

Miami. The U.S. Weather Bureau in Jacksonville, Florida, put out an urgent warning to Jacksonville and southern Floridians to expect high winds the following day. Residents this far south on the Atlantic seaboard were no strangers to hurricanes. They promptly boarded up their windows and prepared for the worst, but the fast-moving storm did them no harm. It was curving north and passed safely off the coast of Jacksonville on the evening of the twentieth. The forecasters, seeing that it was apparently taking a well-known path into the cooler waters off the coast, predicted that it would continue northeast, missing Cape Hatteras off the North Carolina coast, and blow itself out. The forecast referred to it merely as a "Florida cyclone" and was based on the rule that, as hurricanes begin to move over waters cooler than 79 degrees Fahrenheit, they lose their punch and die. Ships, alerted by radio, nevertheless moved out of its anticipated path, which kept them safe but deprived forecasters of updates on the storm's movement.

As ships scattered into port or fled east of its path, reporting on the hurricane largely ceased. Only the Cunard White Star liner *Carinthia*, carrying some six hundred dining and dancing passengers blithely toward a Caribbean adventure, noted GH38's threatening presence on the night of September 20. The captain reported that his barometer had dipped to 27.85 inches, one of the lowest readings ever recorded in the North Atlantic. The storm had tossed his twenty-thousand-ton luxury ship mercilessly in the waves, he reported, and made him wonder if the decks would give way under the weight of the water and the beating it was taking from the relentlessly high seas. However, the *Carinthia* and its passengers and crew rode out the storm, and the next morning the humbled captain sent a message on the teletype that this was one of the most dangerous storms he had ever encountered at sea. Except for his report, and a calculation that it was swooping past Diamond Shoals off Cape Hatteras at 7:30 that morning, the Weather Bureau had no firm fix on GH38.

It was out there, but behaving strangely. Like a cat seeking a warm place to lie, it had centered itself over the warm waters of the Gulf Stream and, contrary to predictions, continued to grow stronger. It cruised north just over the horizon from the eastern seaboard, gathering power and vicious intensity. Slipping up a trough between a high pressure area over the mainland and the Bermuda High to the east, it moved stealthily north. The trough was like a red carpet leading to the shores of Long Island, Connecticut, and Rhode Island, where warm oppressive weather and heavy rains had created the perfect conditions to support its now monstrous appetite and strength.

And then, again like a cat—one that had crept unremarked within striking distance of its prey—the hurricane sprang, sprinting an astounding seven hundred miles over the next twelve hours. New Englanders literally never knew what hit them.

IV

Helen Bengtson was eighteen that summer, happily immersed in her first job out of Amagansett High School on Long Island. With the harsh lessons of the Depression in mind, she had worked diligently in typing and shorthand courses in high school, and the effort had paid off. A petite, hardworking, pretty blonde who showed her Scandinavian ancestry, she had been hired as a secretary to Perry Duryea, owner of the leading lobster business at the eastern end of Long Island, in Amagansett. The Duryea operation included a general store, icehouse, and wholesale lobster business situated on Fort Pond, a protected saltwater pond that spanned almost the entire narrow width of Long Island at one of its narrowest points a few miles west of Montauk. The Fort Pond spilled into Block Island Sound on the north and was separated from the Atlantic by less than a mile on the south side, where a community of fishermen and fishing businesses was nestled into the shore. Her boss, Perry Duryea, was speaker in the New York Assembly and supervisor of East Hampton, but he continued to oversee a lobster business reputed to be the best on the island. It catered to the finer restaurants and shipped lobsters by train to New York City. His wife kept the books for the wholesale business in the office on the big dock at Fort Pond, and Helen kept the records for the store. She earned ten dollars a week.

Helen, at her job in the Duryea store, saw the fishermen, who eked out a leaner existence. Some of them lived in the tarpaper shacks around Fort Pond, even though the ragtag structures weren't substantial enough to serve as year-round housing. Yet overall, she thought they had a good life and, more important, they seemed to think so. Everyone had enough to eat and nobody felt rich or poor, in her opinion. Thrift and frugality were considered virtues by all, and everyone kept an eye out to help their own family. Even schoolchildren scrambled for coal to take home like a prize when the train carrying it threw on its brakes and pieces jolted out onto the tracks from the open heaps in the boxcars.

The biggest part of Helen's job in the Duryea store was keeping track of the barter system in the store, since the fishermen who brought in their catches and worked in the fish factory had credit privileges. Typically their wives came in and did the shopping. It was Helen's job to collect the tabs and keep the records up to date.

Life seemed full of promise to Helen that summer. The fishermen on Long Island were somewhat shielded from the desperate effects of the Depression, which could be seen a few hours' away on the streets of New York where out-of-work men hawked apples and slept in shanties under the El. On Long Island there was always plenty to eat: fish and shellfish and lobster, and vegetables from the garden. Down the road in Southampton and East Hampton, several hundred summer people, mostly New Yorkers and Philadelphians with money, came to cruise in their yachts and show off their wealth and educations, but on eastern Long Island everyone seemed neither rich nor poor. The summer had been a good one for fishing. The introduction of trucks, instead of the daily train run, to carry fish into the city markets showed commercial promise. Up till then, trains would back into the Fort Pond Bay on a big dock with an extension of railroad track long enough for three box-cars. They would pull right up to the boats in the water and take on their loads. But trucks could leave at any time and go directly to the market.

Helen's optimism and good cheer were partly because she was in love and had become engaged that summer to Stuart Vorpahl. Stuart was several years older than she, but they had gone to the same high school together until he graduated. They had hardly noticed each other then. Helen believed it was because in their small school the roll call was alphabetical, and their last names were at different ends of the alphabet. It had been at the annual Montauk lighthouse party the previous New Year's that they had rediscovered each other and, by June, following Helen's graduation, announced their engagement.

Stuart worked that summer for his father, who was a railway express agent, a demanding and important job in a community that received 90 percent of its supplies on the daily train. He wanted to be a fisherman, as did most of the young men on the south fork of Long Island, but unlike his friend Milt Miller, who was born to a fishing family, Stuart had not yet been able to find a reliable job on a commercial or party boat. He didn't really mind unloading the daily train or delivering its shipments at the end of the day, and it became easier when Helen came along to help out. Still, working for the railroad wasn't fishing, and he glanced enviously at the fishermen who came ashore at the end of the day and stood around the fish barrels where they left their catch. Sunburned and windburned, they walked with a bit of swagger, replete in the knowledge of putting in a day's hard work and the male satisfaction of having toiled in nature against the elements.

After work in the Duryea store, Helen often spent her evenings helping Stuart make deliveries off the 7:00 P.M. train. They would run flowers or food, mostly perishables, to the neighboring businesses. The express business was always busier at the beginning and end of summer because East Hampton, five miles away, was mainly a resort town, and the summer people often shipped their household goods, linens, cookware, and even mattresses ahead to their summerhouses by train. In September they were busy with shipping the same goods home as they migrated back to the cities.

The resort business was growing on Long Island. It had developed slowly over the previous eight years of the Depression. Since 1874, farmhouses had advertised to host "people of means" for the summer. That usually meant meeting a family with horse and buggy and showing them a bit of country life, room and board, for several weeks in the

summer to supplement a farming family's income. Farm
wives baked pies and prepared the meals for guests, who
were charmed to see the self-sufficiency of farm life. They
ate vegetables grown in the garden and meat from animals
butchered in the barn. By the 1930s a number of families
rented or owned their own summerhouses on Long Island,
and the tourist industry was growing slowly as a more prosperous economic class began to emerge from the Depression in New York and Philadelphia.

Tuesday night, September 20, Helen had gone down
to the depot to help Stuart after dinner with her parents and
three-year-old brother, Leslie. Before going, she had managed to squeeze in an hour to do some shorthand coaching
for a girlfriend who was eligible for a secretarial job. It
didn't matter that she and Stuart were starting out late to
make the deliveries. It was a beautiful, soft, humid evening
with stars in the sky. Stuart kissed her goodnight when he
dropped her off at home after ten. She remembers that she
wasn't sleepy at all when she finally went to bed, suffused
with the feeling that all was right with the world.

✻ ✻ ✻

Twenty miles west on Long Island, Rick Hendrickson, a
chicken farmer in Bridgehampton, had a few forebodings
about the weather that night. Hendrickson was a weather
bug, everyone agreed. He had always wanted to be a
poultryman and follow in his father's footsteps on their
forty-five-acre Hill View dairy and poultry farm, but some
longing for an academic understanding of science was un-
satisfied in him. When Ernest Clowes, the learned and some-

what introverted observer for the National Weather Bureau who roomed down the lane, appoached Rick's parents about setting up a cooperative weather station in the open potato fields behind the farmhouse, Rick, a high school junior at the time, was intrigued. Sometimes he caddied at the local golf course and made twenty-five cents for twelve holes, but he preferred observing the weather even though it was a nonpaying activity. He quickly convinced Clowes that he could be counted on to take the daily temperature reading and record it for the weather bureau every night at eight. Clowes taught him how to open the shuttered box on a stand and stay far enough away from the thermometer so that no puff of breath might change the reading. He also sternly instructed Rick to never hold the recording pencil when he flipped the wheel carrying the thermometer so he would get a fresh reading the following day. Too often, Clowes warned, the wheel would snap around quickly, flip the thermometer into the pencil, and break. Rick was careful, and in 1931 he became an official cooperative observer for the bureau. He could mail in the daily meteorological records on his own.

On the Hendrickson chicken farm, debt was a way of life, as it was to most farmers. Rick understood that every dollar his father made was committed to the bank, the feed store, and the lumber store, but there was a bounty of food and good living on the farm just the same. He hunted with his grandfather for ducks. They lobstered and made wild cherry rum, and throughout the leanest years of the Depression they dined on asparagus, raspberries, cabbage, peas, and beans, all grown in the garden and canned by his mother and grandmother. They cured their own pigs by hanging them in the barn and butchered the cows as they needed them. Even after the Depression ended, the Hendricksons, with equal amounts of pride and humility, were proud to say they never knew what hunger was.

On Tuesday night, September 20, Rick was getting ready for a busy following day. A professor from Cornell University was coming to certify the family flock of leghorn chickens. The Hendricksons considered them the crown of the Long Island poultry business. Rick, his father, the professor, and an assistant would catch and examine every one of the three hundred birds. They would look for a certain hue in each bird's dark pupil and for orange irises, note whether the bird complied with the four-and-a-half-pound body build for the breed, and check to see that there were no feathers on their legs. Then they would take blood samples and put a band on each chicken's leg. Only after that could the hatchery be certified as having a pure and approved leghorn flock. Rick knew it would be a long and tedious day. The sticky weather wouldn't make it any easier. Before he checked the thermometer in the stand, he looked out over the potato fields. He loved Long Island and understood how the painter Thomas Moran, who worked on Long Island, had come to paint it, to replicate the soft rural scenes and the big sky coming down to the coast. He had just heard on the radio that rain was expected on the southern coastline of New Jersey, with winds of 25 miles an hour. Based on his recent readings in meteorology, that sounded like a tropical storm. But he was just guessing. He took his measurement, turned the wheel carefully, and went to bed.

❊ ❊ ❊

In Southampton at Grassmere, the old, three-story Victorian house built at the turn of the century on Lake Agawam and now host to three generations of Lees, life moved at a different pace, one that reached back fifteen years to evoke memories of F. Scott Fitzgerald's Southampton. It was a free-spirited, fashionable world of open convertibles, fur-collared coats, yacht club parties, and sometimes impulsive, reckless fun. Thanks to the gregarious and generous nature of the patriarch of the family, James Parrish Lee, a respected international lawyer, Grassmere was a frequent center of summer social activities in Southampton, including the Fourth of July party where guests watched the fireworks over the lake. Cocktails—martinis crisp, cold, and dry, in particular—were routinely served to family and friends at six o'clock. Granddaughter Lee Lawrence, ten, normally played backgammon in the evening while the grown-ups shook their drinks in that most adult of cocktail accoutrements, in the grandchildrens' opinion, a cocktail shaker. Its prestige rivaled their grandfather's famous Buddha from Japan, which he brought to the grand dining table. When it faced them, they were expected to be silent and listen to the adults. When he turned it to face him, they were free to talk and ask questions.

Lee was anxious that summer. Even though the adults hushed their conversation about the chance of war in Europe when the children were within earshot, she had picked up enough eavesdropping to know there was trouble in the world. At night she had nightmares of trying to escape from Nazi troops, and even the comfort of her grandfather's spacious house with four servants and the fabulous rectangular "bamboo room," where he kept his collection of memorabilia from around the world, could assuage her anxieties. Despite their family's wealth, her mother and aunt kept strict household accounts and sometimes spent hours tallying, to the amusement of other family members, which of them owed 20 or 30 cents to the food budget. But there was always fun, too. On weekend afternoons the family went about its favorite new pastime. They teed up on their lawn and tried to drive golf balls across Lake Agawam.

❖ ❖ ❖

The end of summer often comes late in coastal New England. Good weather extends the pleasures of summer well into September, and in the thirties, school typically didn't start until the first of October. The water stayed warm and skies were clear, causing many to lament that the best weather invariably settled in when it was time to go home. Families who "summered" often chose to return their children back to school late in order to linger for a few last stolen days of summer.

The summer of 1938 had been hot, sultry, humid, and wet on Long Island. The Driver family from Newark, New Jersey, saw no reason to abandon the seaside at Westhampton to return to New Jersey quite yet. Newark would be hot and sticky, and Frank Driver was not anxious to get back. He had brought his family to their summerhouse on Beach Lane across from the Hampton Inn with the primary aim of resting and pulling himself together after a difficult year. He had arrived emotionally spent. His businesss had suffered the previous year, and when one of his Westhampton neighbors dropped dead of a heart attack and another died of pneumonia, he spiraled into depression. But by September his spirits were beginning to improve, and on September 21 he planned to take his wife Louise and their son out fishing in their twenty-five-foot Jersey sea skiff, the *Black Duck*. Their daughter Patricia, ten, didn't like to fish, so Louise had phoned their friend Tot Greene to see if Patricia could go to the Greene's house the next afternoon. Tot, who was already looking for something to amuse her two children since rain seemed likely, seized the opportunity to create an end-of-season occasion for the children. She invited Patricia and the neighboring Bradley children to come for lunch.[2]

Patricia and her friend Gretchen were sorry to see the end of summer arrive. Their summer had passed as gloriously and quickly as usual. They had played Monopoly and cards and listened to the radio at night and were allowed to stay up well past what was their bedtime during the school year. Life was relaxed, but with a few social conventions strictly observed. The children ate supper separately from the adults on the side porch while their parents sat at the table in the dining room, often tended by the cook and chambermaid. Shoes were required at dinner. Patricia's father played piano, and that summer he had immersed himself in the healing qualities of his music with added fervor. He was fond of popular tunes, and she lay in bed drifting to sleep many nights that summer listening to the strains of the popular new song, "Deep Purple."

Much about the summer had been idyllic for the grown-ups, too: sailing Saturdays and Sundays at the Quantuck Beach Club, Saturday night dances, and the occasional junior league follies and amateur hours. Most mornings began at the beach and then moved to sailing, golf, or tennis after lunch. The children floated alongside in a soft satellite world of helpful servants, sporting lessons, freshly laundered clothes, and social arrangements. They were cosseted by attentive adults and yet beneficiaries of the space and freedom and play that were granted to children in a culture that clearly delineated between the worlds of adults and of children. No one spoke in front of them about the war rumbling in Europe or the suffering of some at home during the Depression. They were taught and understood that excess was bad and to be avoided, that there were others who had less than themselves, and that displays of wealth were unseemly. They were granted the great inestimable gift of childhood: ignorance of the adult concerns that would enter their lives soon enough.

✿ ✿ ✿

Adams Nickerson was up early Wednesday morning at the other end of Long Island, Oyster Bay. His father's chauffeur was going to drive him to Grand Central Station in Manhattan so he could catch the noon train back to school. Because this was his second year at St. Mark's preparatory school in Southborough, Massachusetts, where he would be starting the ninth grade, Adams felt like a practiced traveler. Other things made him feel more grown-up this year. He had to keep track of the fifty dollars, tucked away safely in his suit jacket pocket, that his father's secretary had given him for the trip. He was carrying his tennis racket and his camera. And then there was the new three-piece brown suit that he wore proudly.

At breakfast his mother mentioned that there was going to be a rainstorm, but there was nothing unusual in that, he thought. He just hoped he wouldn't get his suit wet.

By the time he had settled into his seat in one of the last four Pullman cars on the Bostonian, the express train that linked the larger cities of the Northeast, he was relieved to be on his way. There was a hint of fun and liberation in the air on the train. Many of the passengers, boys like himself, were also headed back to school, and for the duration of the trip they were on their own away from home. He recognized a few older boys in the car in front and knew they would be on the bus that would meet them at Framingham to take them to St. Mark's. The train traveled along the coast through New York and Connecticut. Adams caught glimpses of the rough water and whitecaps in Long Island Sound as the Bostonian moved out through Mamaroneck and Rye.

* * *

People in seaside communities from New York to Maine went about their business as usual that Wednesday morning, as did Emily Fowler in Old Lyme, Connecticut. She was not to be deterred by a little rough weather. Her summer wasn't over yet. Classes didn't start at the Chapin School in New York City until October. When a boyfriend, Atwood Ely, called to suggest that they go out sailing, she jumped at the chance. The wind was a little high, they remarked, but they both knew how to sail the small knockabout boat, a little sloop with a centerboard that Atwood kept at Griswold Point at the mouth of the Connecticut River. They thought it would be exciting to sail in such wind. They listened to the radio on the drive down, with an ear out for storm warnings, but there was no weather report. It was lightly raining when they put the sails up and set out on the water at eleven.

※ ※ ※

Up in Fenwick, Connecticut, the actress Katharine Hepburn was spending a morning exemplary of life along the New England coast. She loved the big, old Victorian house, built in 1870, that belonged to her parents and described it to anyone who asked as her idea of paradise. Fenwick, forty-five miles from Hartford at the mouth of the Connecticut River, was strictly a summer colony and typically deserted by late September, but Kate loved the feeling of emptiness. She had been coming here since she was six, and in spite of her glamorous acting career, existence in Fenwick was the way she believed real life should be. Now she was licking her wounds after being hailed as box office poison following a series of unsuccessful films. Her career was in a temporary slump.

She went for her usual morning swim at eight, enjoying the light breeze and clear air. The colors seemed especially distinct. After breakfast she noticed that a steady wind was blowing, but it still looked like a good day to play golf, which was her plan. Out on the golf course, she and her partner Red Hammond could see that the wind was getting stronger. She was ecstatic on the par-three ninth when her drive rolled in for a hole-in-one. She shot a brilliant thirty-one on the nine holes, which was her record. They were hot after playing in the high humidity and decided to go home and take a swim to celebrate.[3]

* * *

The weather looked even clearer that morning further north, in Westerly, Rhode Island. Rev. G. Edgar Tobin of the Christ Episcopal Church was looking forward to his day. He and his son Jack, home from Yale Medical School, had been bacheloring it for a few days while his wife was on trip to Canada. Today was the annual meeting of the ten-member Christ Episocpal Church Mother's Club, and he was to officiate at a special Communion service for the group at ten, followed by lunch. He knew that the carrot and egg salad sandwiches, in keeping with the club's low budget, would be made already. The women of the Mothers' Club were some of his favorite congregants. They gave their time and energy to the church's charity efforts and set a cheerful tone for church social events. Some, like Mae Lowry, who lived around the corner from the rectory, were also neighbors. He had accepted the group's invitation to go down to the Lowry beachfront cottage at Misquamicut for a picnic after the service, but he would have to leave promptly after lunch to perform a funeral at 2:00 PM back at church. An early riser, he typically ran over the schedule for the day ahead while he shaved. This morning he also mused that it was the first time in the women's group's ten-year history that his wife, a member of the club, would miss the annual festivities. It had always been a fun afternoon for the women, a respite for several who led rather quiet and purposeful, though uneventful lives, helping with their extended families and working at home during the Depression.

V

The summer of 1938 was the best summer eight-year-old Cathy Moore could remember. In early June her family had moved the seven miles from their home in Westerly, Rhode Island, down to their summerhouse on Napatree Point, where gracious summerhouses stretched out into Long Island Sound. Theirs was a three-story gray shingle house with a steeply sloped roof, boxy front dormers, and servants' quarters in the attic that her father had built two summers before. It was considered the most substantially built of the "cottages" on the Fort Road toward the point, an L-shaped spit of land extending three miles from Rhode Island's lacy coastline like a crab's leg. Like other houses along Fort Road, the Moore house perched just a few steps behind a low seawall that enabled residents to live as close to the water as possible. Cathy, her older sister Anne, brother Geoffrey, and little sister Margaret looked forward more to moving down to the shore in summer than to anything else in their young lives, including Christmas.

The house was a place where they could truly run free and relax, and though a summerhouse was quite a luxury in the late years of the Depression, their mother Catherine kept it simply furnished. She subscribed to a "plainer is richer" philosophy of the time that considered the plain wicker furniture, woven grass rugs, and summer chintz slipcovers to be smart. The family cook and laundress accompanied the Moores to the beach in summer, but Catherine painstakingly packed her kitchen utensils herself and brought them with her. She would have thought it extravagant to purchase duplicates, and at the beginning of summer she had sent her cook back into town to collect the potato peeler that she had left at home in the kitchen drawer.

While just a few minutes separated the Moores' year-round home on fashionable Elm Street in Westerly and the summerhouse on Napatree Point, a world of difference existed between life in the two places. One of the reasons Cathy and her two sisters and brother loved summer life was that it had a liberating effect on their mother. They could tell by her easy laughter and manner when she was there that she loved it, too, and she typically kept them at the beach as late into the fall as she could, until the weather got too cold to stay. A potbellied woodstove that burned charcoal briquets held off the autumn chill.

Catherine was proper, efficient, and reserved, as befit the wife of a successful manufacturing plant owner in Westerly. It was she who maintained a sense of decorum with the household servants while her husband Jeff on occasion found his way back down to the kitchen after dinner to eat fudge, as his girth suggested, and chat with the help. He was gregarious and charmed the workers in his elastics mill with his down-to-earth good nature. They laughed when he tried to talk them out of the pepper-and-egg sandwiches they brought for lunch. In summer, Catherine still supervised the help with an efficient manner and kept a sharp eye out to see that the young maids reported home in the evening by nine o'clock, but in private she let down her guard. She and her children laughed at the grand old ladies who were chauffeured from the yacht club to their nearby houses after their martini lunches. She delighted in the true old characters like Mrs. Helen Joy Lee, who swam in the bay every morning wearing her rubber swim cap with a thermometer between her teeth to enable her to report the water temperature to the neighbors.

So long as the weather stayed warm enough for the potbellied stove to keep them warm, the Moores willingly stayed late to savor the last of summer's halcyon days. The weather had been glorious but for a few days of rain and humidity. The crisp, sharp, clear days that heralded the turning of the season hadn't come yet. Cathy and her sister Anne rode into school in Westerly with their father on his way to work and were picked up and brought back to Napatree by one of the servants or extended family members at the end of the day. Except for the change in routine, it still felt like summer.

That summer Cathy had taken her new parrot, Polly, out to Napatree along with the family dog, Major, and a cat that was expecting kittens before Labor Day. She had earned the parrot from her Aunt Harriet for not biting her fingernails in a contest with her cousin Mary. Despite her parents' reservations about adding a bird to an already full household of children, pets, and household help, her aunt had kept her word and bought Cathy a parrot when she won.

In July, Cathy sat to have her portrait painted. She had taken swimming lessons off the dock behind the house and was able to swim a mile by Labor Day. She had also taken horseback lessons in nearby Shelter Harbor, and the sum of so many new activities and so much fun prompted her to announce that the closing summer had been "wonderful." That was the night of Tuesday, September 20, when she began to experience the onset of that creeping, heavy feeling that summer was coming to a quick end. Her brother Geoffrey's clothes were laid out to pack for his second year at boarding school. It had been raining for several days, the surest sign that summer would soon come to an end, and the Moore children understood that as soon as the weather changed and the days gradually became shorter, they would be moving home. Catherine came to the girls' bedroom and sat down on Cathy's bed with the fluffy pink blanket covers. They talked about the weather in hopes that the next day would be clear so the children could play outside after school and so Catherine could hang out the laundry. Catherine had sent them out in the rain to gather Irish sea moss for the cook to boil down as a thickener for pudding that afternoon, but the girls already suspected that it was mostly a ploy to get them out of the house. Catherine told them that the Providence newspaper was not predicting bad weather. The weather was a constant topic of conversation at this time of year, when the line storms that formed offshore and the autumnal high tides they called moontides

created a little drama and an exciting sense of seasonal
change. New Englanders both at the beach and inland
often went to the shore to observe them.

"What is a typoon?" asked Anne, who followed her
mother's explanation with another question. "What is a hurricane?" Catherine explained as best she could that they
were big rainstorms with high winds. "But we don't have
them here," she said. "Hurricanes don't come to New England." Then she kissed them goodnight and turned out the
light.

Another family named Moore, though no relation to the Jeff
Moore family of Westerly, had owned a cottage on Napatree
Point for twenty years. The summer of 1938, Paul Moore
and his neighbor Jim Nestor discussed how they missed
seeing a high surf. They loved watching the big waves breaking against the seawalls, especially at high tide. Their houses
on Fort Road sat only six or seven feet above high water,
but they felt safe behind the seawalls, even when the high tide
in Watch Hill was five feet high and the waves broke thirty
to forty feet closer to shore in front of their homes. They also
knew that Napatree Point had been thickly wooded before
the Great Gale of 1815 that took out every tree and the only .
cottage on Napatree at the time. Paul and his wife Audrey
occasionally discussed the possibility that such a storm could
happen again, but they had confidence that the seawalls
would hold and protect their property.

When Paul and Audrey and their eleven-year-old son
returned to Schenectady on Labor Day, Paul's father, stepmother, and sister Havila, from Staten Island, came to enjoy

September, their favorite time to be at the seashore. Paul's father returned to work in New York City on Monday morning, September 19, and left his wife and Havila, who was handicapped by a hip malformation and could not walk without holding on to a rail since she refused to use crutches or a wheelchair, to close up the cottage in the middle of the week. He would be back to pick them up and take them home on Thursday, September 22.[4]

Forty miles farther north, in Providence, a nervous bride and her mother were being bedeviled by the weather. They were readying for an elegant evening wedding in the Narragansett Hotel downtown. Lorraine Martin and her fiancé, Josef Fogel, had chosen the Narragansett after deciding that a judge would be best to perform their ceremony. The Fogels were Jewish and Lorraine was Christian, so a temple or church wedding wasn't an option. Their families did not object. Josef was twenty-five and Lorraine was also in her twenties. They both earned their own money, a real accomplishment in 1938, and were clearly adults. And as anyone could see, they were madly in love. The tall, handsome Josef, who was partial to double-breasted suits, and stylish, soft-featured Lorraine made a striking couple around Providence. Lorraine, who worked as an interior decorator and had started her own jewelry company, had flair. Josef worked in his father's beer distribution company. The society editor of the *Providence Journal* was covering the wedding for the paper. It was the kind of item that Depression readers, many of whom worked downtown or in the mills, liked; a story that smacked of romance and local glamour. The society pages, like the movies, were bits of entertainment they could afford to enjoy and live through vicariously.

The forecast for rain, "heavy at times," made Lorraine anxious about parking for her guests. She was also worried about the incoming train schedules, especially for Judge Maurice Robinson, who was going to perform the ceremony and lived in outlying Providence. Her greatest concern was that her dress, a three-quarter-length tulle evening gown copied from the glamorous dresses worn by the actress Joan Bennett in the movies, might get soaked after the wedding when she and Josef left for the Biltmore Hotel down the street. They had intended to ride in Josef's Plymouth convertible with the rumble seat. She was keeping her fingers crossed that it wouldn't rain until after the wedding, but because of the increasing wind, she and her mother decided to go to the Narragansett Hotel early to avoid any traffic problems later and to keep an eye on the arrangements in the dining room. They were barely out the door when the phone rang.

Her mother put her hand over the receiver. "It's Miss Dyer from the *Journal*," she whispered. Lorraine rolled her eyes and took the receiver. "Yes, we're going on with it. We're headed downtown now," she told her calmly.

* * *

Several fisherman who had seen two coppery sunrises in succession decided to stay in that day. The West Indian wife of a Portuguese fisherman in Warwick, Rhode Island, prevailed upon her husband to not go out that morning. She said she didn't like the goofy way the birds were acting, just as she had seen them do before hurricanes in the Caribbean. Her husband thought she was superstitious, but he finally gave in and stayed home.

There were other signs for anyone who put store in animal behavior. In Sakonnet in eastern Rhode Island, farmers noticed that the cows ate and then lay down again. Wild ducks circled in the sky and stopped. Some said they thought the horses in the fields were acting kind of wild. In Providence, it was remarked that the waterfront rats were moving inland. There seemed to be more of them inland, people remarked, especially atop the city's downtown hills.

❃ ❃ ❃

There were no such portents for Aclon Coggeshall in Narragansett, twenty miles up the southern coast of Rhode Island from the Moore family on Napatree Point. At half past seven every morning, Aclon went to work at the exclusive Dunes Beach Club. To Rhode Islanders, the Dunes Club was top among venerable old-shoe beach clubs, both elegant and rustic. The rolling surf and gently tapering shoreline were reputed to make it the best beach in Rhode Island, and famous dance bands played there on summer nights for the aristocratic membership.

Aclon's work was just barely slowing down for fall, but the number of social events had tapered off after Labor Day. That summer a new casino had opened in Narragansett with a dance hall, and the big bands, like Johnny Miller's, had been major attractions. Just about everyone, it seemed, put on a coat and tie and went to the dances on weekends. Yachters who came onto Tucker's dock could hear the music wafting across the water as year-round locals and the fashionable summer residents took their turns on the dance floor.

The term in Narragansett was "quiet money." That was how Aclon Coggeshall and the locals referred to the wealthy summer residents from New York and Philadelphia who frequented the Dunes Club and the Point Judith Country Club, one of the oldest golf clubs in America. No one with any taste or breeding flaunted their riches during the Depression, and in fact, in New England, a lack of ostentation and overall thriftiness were considered Yankee virtues even in good times. Summer people, no matter how deep their pockets, reveled in simplicity while on vacation, and by prevailing standards knew how to play down their wealth and to relax. Many a Philadelphia heiress went to the town rummage sales in summer coastal communities, and it was considered good breeding to avoid any display of extravagance. Their homes were comfortable but seldom overdecorated, and the best of the summer residents, in the minds of the locals, showed no pretentions in their relationship with the community. There was little tension between locals and summer people in Narragansett.

Aclon, who also worked delivering groceries, was impressed with summer residents like Isaac Emerson, known as "the Bromo-Seltzer king" because his fortune was derived from his invention of the headache remedy, Bromo-Seltzer. Emerson invited Aclon to step in and have a cup of coffee with him at the kitchen table when he made his deliveries.

Narragansett called itself "America's Peerless Watering Place." The smooth coastline without barrier beaches or dunes offered clean views northeast to Newport and south-

west to Block Island on a clear day. Aclon was twenty-three
that fall and looked a bit like a young Charlton Heston, tall
and broad-shouldered with an immaculate smile, as he went
about his work as a beachboy at the Dunes Club. He was
about as native as you could get in Rhode Island. His an-
cestors had come to America soon after the *Mayflower*. His
great-grandfather had been the first president of the Colony
of Rhode Island in 1647.

On the morning of September 21, he set to work opening up the cabanas and hanging out the beach towels and
setting up the furniture at the Dunes. Members routinely
arrived late morning, stayed for lunch, and went home in
the afternoon. Some stayed to play cards and swim in the
afternoon. But on Wednesday, the bathhouse manager, Ben
Curtis, was watching the weather. The wind was increasing
gradually, and he wondered if they'd soon have to start bringing things inside. He told Aclon to be ready if the weather
got worse.

School was already in session six miles across the bay in
Jamestown, Rhode Island. The children had climbed on to
the bus that morning that would deliver them to the local
middle and elementary schools. It seemed too nice a day,
sunny but with a haze, to have to go to school when the
beach still beckoned. But as the bus traveled the causeway
between the two halves, like lobes connected by a narrow
crosspiece, to Conanicut Island, there were long, rolling
waves and whitecaps dancing out on the bay below them.

VI

Out of sight offshore, GH38 had by now become a Category Four storm, with winds blowing 131 to 155 miles per hour. Yet as it headed north, it caused only bluster and dampness along the mid-Atlantic coastline, not enough to set off warnings for the placid coastal communities of Long Island and adjacent New England.

Without satellite pictures, weather prediction was an inexact science. Even with reports of wind speeds, temperatures, and barometric readings from ships at sea, analysis of such data and ways to alert the public were inefficient. It could take from three to six hours for meteorologists to gather and analyze the the data in Morse code messages that teletype operators tapped out from ships at sea. It might be even longer before the news found its way to the public by radio or the next newspaper edition, by which time the storm could have arrived — or changed course completely. Old-timers who read the intensity of a storm by watching long swells and timing the duration between them as they hit the shore did almost as well in predicting when a storm would arrive.

There had been no report on GH38 since the captain of the *Carinthia*'s portentous message that morning, and forecasters at the Weather Bureau found no cause for alarm. They were certain the hurricane would turn and blow out to sea rather than head inland. Everyone but Charlie Pierce.

When the storm moved north of Florida, responsibility for its reporting shifted from Jacksonville, Florida, to the auspices of the bureau in Washington, D.C. The bureau chiefs concurred that the hurricane would move east rather than north, as did most coastal disturbances at this latitude, where the prevailing west-to-east winds drove them seaward. One junior forecaster in Washington, Charlie Pierce, twenty-eight, disagreed. At the midday bureau meeting on September 21, Pierce explained his prediction that a strong high-pressure system in the North Atlantic would keep the hurricane from moving away. He drew a chart that showed the narrow low-pressure trough that would guide the storm to New England and showed the hurricane striking at Long Island, maybe even traveling north, but his colleagues scoffed at the idea.

His forecast was discounted for several reasons. Pierce was junior and substituting for a senior forecaster who was on vacation that day. His superiors thought he might be trying too hard to declare a crisis. After all, he had been with the bureau less than a year, and his chart and prediction were disregarded. One of the chief forecasters asserted that the odds were 100 to 1 that the hurricane would peter out and head to sea. Pierce argued that there was no opening in the position of the Bermuda High, positioned ten degrees' higher north latitude than usual. It had the hurricane blocked from going east. There simply wasn't an opening, and a second weather front from the west over the mainland barricaded its western access. The bosses shrugged. They did not think a major hurricane was probable, and the fact that only two had been recorded in New England in the previous three hundred years seemed to support their theory. So the Weather Bureau issued mild warnings, and the major regional newspapers in the Northeast forecast only, "Rain, heavy at times." Yet in 1635 and 1815, hurricanes believed to be as great as GH38 had hit the area, also ushered in by warm tropical air and rains, and trailing tidal surges. Such hurricanes were rare but not unheard-of, though most meteorologists at the time did not hearken back to Plymouth Plantation and the Great Colonial Hurricane (1635), or even back 123 years ago to the Great September Gale of 1815 when making predictions. Though recorded in histories, they had been almost forgotten, and after the storm the acting chief of the Weather Bureau even went so far as to excuse the bureau's erroneous forecast because, he claimed, GH38 "did not follow the usual pattern. . . ." When in fact, it did.

Charlie Pierce may have been sure of his prediction or he may have gambled and gotten lucky. Meteorologists at the time knew very little of the upper atmosphere, thirty thousand feet and above, where most cloud formations and weather conditions begin. With no means to chart the strong westerly winds that we know today as the jet stream, Pierce may have credited the steering currents around the Bermuda High for driving GH38 north to New England when instead the jet stream was responsible. It seems just as likely to modern meteorologists that the jet stream in that period was looping up northeast along the coast and ushered the hurricane north. But there were no methods at the time to chart those steering currents at the top of the weather system.

By midmorning, outer bands of the storm began to reach Long Island. Like a big cat slapping teasingly at a mouse with the back of its paw, it flung playful gusts and showers, interspersed with calm periods, ahead against the low, sandy shores. Just one hundred miles to the south, it sideswiped the New Jersey shore with gale-force wind and waves. Fourteen blocks of scenic boardwalk were torn up in Manasquan. The pounding rain inflicted severe damage on the thirty-three-thousand acre tomato crop from Cape May to Sussex. Close to half the apple crop, a source of pride to agricultural New Jersey, was also damaged as the wind and rain broke the boughs off and uprooted thousands of trees in ground already wet from several previous days of rain. One farmer's flock of four thousand pheasants panicked in North Haledon, New Jersey, in the high winds. A thousand of them smothered before their owner could pry them apart.

But incredibly, by today's hyperquick standards of weather reporting, no one seemed to draw the conclusion that these winds, topping out at about 65 miles an hour, might be a harbinger of something bigger. It was a mere gale that slowed commuter traffic. Wind caused pedestrians to hang on to parking meters and lampposts for support. It tore off some marquees and left a scattering of business signs dangling dangerously. Over the horizon to the southeast, a hundred miles offshore, the center of the storm was moving at an unheard-of 60 miles per hour, aimed straight at Long Island. The big cat had only played, so far. The Weather Bureau predicted heavy rain for Long Island and the Connecticut–Rhode Island coastline as GH38 headed for the most densely populated coastal area in the country.

VII

George Burghard and his wife Mabel were in their rental cottage on Dune Road in Westhampton, where they'd spent the summer. George was a retired radio research engineer, and he chose the cottage facing out to sea so he could, without interference, conduct radio experiments from two poles over fifty feet high that supported radio antennae on the adjacent empty lot. Their cottage was roughly equidistant from the beach dunes at the waterfront and Dune Road, about one hundred feet behind it. The Coast Guard station lay west of them on the other side of the vacant lot. Sand dunes higher than a man added to the feeling of protection from the ocean at high tide, but what Mabel and George Burghard liked was the cottage's proximity to the water, so they could watch breakers crash on the beach and challenge the dunes in a storm.

Mabel was robust and undaunted by a little rough weather. She liked sports. She swam and played tennis, and in her youth had been one of the country's first woman race-car drivers. She and George had planned to leave home about noon for Forest Hills, where the national singles tennis championships were being played, and spend the night in the city. Selma and Carl Dalin, the couple who worked as their housekeeper and caretaker in Westhampton, would stay behind in the beach house until the Burghards returned.

Around eleven o'clock, Mabel heard on the radio that wind and rain had caused the tennis matches to be canceled, so she and George decided to wait until the next day to go into the city. She called her friend Tot Greene, who lived two miles away on Dune Road, to tell her they'd decided not to leave until the next day. Tot had a house full of children as well as her in-laws, and she remarked that it looked like they were in for a real storm. She wished it would hurry up and pass through so the children could go outside. Patricia Driver and her friends the Bradley kids had just arrived, and her mother-in-law and her two friends were about to settle into their regular bridge game. Tot and the maid were preparing lunch. Every week her husband came out by train from his office in New York City on Wednesday, and she usually drove to the train station to pick him up. Her eye was on the clock, knowing that the day would be full with its various agendas. The wind was blowing so hard that Marian Bradley wanted the children to come to Tot's at the shore rather than play in the village, where she worried that blowing objects posed a real danger to the children. She had already watched a limb blow off the elm tree in their yard and a road sign come dancing on the wind into the lawn.

Tot had her eye on the ocean out the window. Theirs was the last house on the west end of the barrier beach, on the bay side of Dune Road. Storms were exciting, but what she wanted most at the moment was for the sun to come out so the children could go outside.

The Burghards exulted in the storm despite having to cancel their trip to Forest Hills. The surf the previous afternoon was the highest they had ever seen it. George's cousin had come over to watch it with him. He intended to come again on Wednesday. The wind had started strong from the north that morning, but the surf didn't seem as high as it had been the day before. The morning was hot and sultry, and a light rain began in the late morning. By 11:30 the wind was shifting east and picking up. George was settling in for a good northeaster, those powerful storms that run up the coast of New England with winds from the northeast, and the sport of watching the high surf break against the eight-foot-high dunes in front of the house. Mabel, less of a weather aficionado than her engineer husband, gathered her sewing and settled in on the sunporch with her back to the windows.

The Dalins stayed in servants' rooms in the basement. Just before noon, Carl Dalin spotted water bubbling up through the concrete floor of the Burghards' garage. He and George assumed it was bay water backing up in the wind. The Burghard house was extremely well constructed on a concrete foundation. A sturdy wooden bulkhead lay between it and the ocean. The central living area was on the second story with an ocean view above the dunes. At first, George wasn't overly concerned by the leakage, but then he tasted the water. It was salty, but because no waves had come over the dunes, he guessed that the water had seeped through the sand.

Just the same, he turned the radio on to station WEAF to get the time signals he used to set his chronometer and the weather report. The station said that the West Indies hurricane that had been off Cape Hatteras seemed to be changing course and could conceivably hit Long Island. The tone of the announcer was so offhand that George hardly took notice. Anyway, he considered the idea of a hurricane on Long Island to be ridiculous.[5]

❊ ❊ ❊

Helen Bengston had walked the quarter mile home for lunch, and between the wind and the rain she had decided to wear her raincoat back to work. Perry and Mrs. Duryea had left earlier in the day for a meeting in New York City and put Helen in charge of the store and the office. There had been an air of excitement in the store all morning as she overheard the fishermen talking about a nor'easter coming. By midmorning, those who hadn't gone out already had decided to move their boats to the more protected harbors of Lake Montauk and Gosman Pond. But there were two brothers in the store who couldn't make up their minds what to do. They debated whether to go and get their boats or to leave them where they were, out in open water. One argued that it would be more prudent to bring them into the smaller, protected harbor of Fort Pond. The other said this blow wasn't going to be harder than any other nor'easter and they should take their chances. Nearly an hour passed as they stood around drinking coffee and talking about it. By the time they came to the conclusion that it would be better to move the boats, the storm was under way. Buttoning up their oiled jackets and snugging their hats on their heads, they stepped outside. Already the wind was too high to wear a hat, even a fisherman's slant-brimmed hat with a chin strap. Determined now to move the boats, they headed out into the storm. They knew that moving the boats would be a fight.

Helen was not someone who worried about things. She was alone in her office at the end of the store after the brothers left, but she wasn't unduly concerned. Out the window she could see that men out between the icehouse and the general store and lobster pounds were scurrying around trying to tie everything down in the wind. She returned to matters on her desk until the howling wind began to make the general store building shake. Some of the canned goods started flying off the shelves and Helen had a laugh to herself, thinking, if this is a big storm, I'm not going to drown but be killed by cans of sauerkraut flying through the air. She was also thinking that maybe she should clear the tops of her desk and Perry Duryea's, so their papers didn't get blown and shuffled around, when the phone rang. It was her mother. She was concerned that Helen's father had left home with her brother, three-year-old Leslie, to go bring his two boats around to Lake Montauk, a more sheltered small harbor in the storm. Helen could sense another note of anxiety in her mother's voice. Their house was a quarter of a mile from the water, and storms made her worry about flooding since she didn't swim. Just as Helen was about to suggest that her mother come meet her at the store, the line went dead. The lights in the store also went out.

At roughly the same time, 2:40, an observer for the Weather Bureau in Bridgehampton telephoned the New York office of the bureau and asked for permission to spread warnings of what looked to him like a severe gale, but just as he was granted his request, his telephone went dead, too. It was the same story throughout Long Island. Montauk had installed phone service within the year, but it was a fragile system and cranky under the best conditions. Now the phone lines were blown down. With no electricity, phone, or telegraph service, the coastline ahead, across the sound, could not be alerted. It was too late.[6]

Perry Duryea's brother-in-law Stuart had been left in charge of the icehouse and other operations. He, too, was tying down everything in the fish house, in the store, and on the dock. Some of the fish boxes and lobster traps, open, cagelike affairs, were already flying through the air. Helen watched Stuart drive a tractor-trailer into the space between the store and the wholesale building so it would be protected if the water came up. He also drove his brand-new car, a Cadillac he was crazy about, around the corner and parked it next to the icehouse, a big building, for shelter. Helen was looking out the window when all of a sudden the icehouse blew apart and one entire side of it fell in one piece on Stuart's new car. She saw shingles, signs, lobster boxes, and anything else that wasn't tied down blowing through the air. A few moments later, several of the burly French Canadians who worked for Duryea came through the door to get her. With one man on each side of her, five-foot-two and 115 pounds, she would not blow away in the gusts, now up to 90 miles per hour. The three of them, the men holding tightly to

Helen, ran the fifty feet up the hill to the Duryea house, where anyone left on the Fort Pond dock headed for refuge.

* * *

Further inland, in Bridgehampton, the inspection of the leghorn chickens had gone routinely on the Hendrickson chicken farm. The day began with fog, drizzle, and a tropical sort of feeling to it. After lunch served in the farmhouse by his mother and grandmother, Rick, his father, and the inspectors returned to the poultry buildings. "Goddamn, this is a helluva wind," Dr. Stockey, the vet, had remarked with a toothpick between his teeth as they headed out. "Goddamn, this is a nor'easter," echoed one of the laborers. The wind had really picked up, and Rick thought of his wife Dorothea, who had driven into Bridgehampton to work that morning. She was not the type to stay home and be a farmwife, even though she had had to give up her teaching job when she married him. She was a good driver and always kept her wits about her, so he figured the wind, a nor'easter even, wouldn't be a problem for her. The wind had begun blowing hard now, but it was almost a relief from the sticky stillness that had preceded it. The men went back to their business with the chickens, ignoring the weather, until they saw the roof of the twenty-by-eighty-foot poultry building they were standing in begin to rise and fall. They could look under the post at the corner of the building and see that the rod that held the post to the concrete was moving.

It looked unsafe, so they left the chicken house and fought their way through the orchard back to the farmhouse. Rick saw that two of the five poultry houses had already blown away. The chickens being housed in them were completely gone. Only a pipe remained where there had been an automatic fountain for the fowl. The apples and pears in the orchard littered the ground like jewels. They watched as the brick chimney from the farmhouse kitchen was blown over. Rick's father had taken out a loan that spring for some Johns Manville shingles for the house roof because the salesman had attested, "They will never blow off." Now the shingles were blowing around them in dangerous profusion. The farm was well enough back from the water so that the rising sea wasn't a worry to Rick, but the monstrous strength of the winds was what he feared. He watched as the wind blew down another chicken house and hurled the white chickens into the fence at the edge of the property and held them tightly to the fence like so many newspapers pinned against each strand. In the birds' panic and the rain that followed, every last chicken in the prize flock died.

In Westhampton, George Burghard noted that despite the 90 mile an hour winds he estimated, there was no surf coming over the dunes in front of the house. It was 2:00 P.M. He had stepped outside to right and fasten an antenna for his radio equipment that the wind had blown down. Once he was back in the house, he decided to call and tell his cousin Bill that it was blowing so hard that he thought he should stay home. He was worried about Bill having trouble keeping his car on the road in such strong winds. When he tried to call, the phone was dead. So it came as a surprise when it rang ten minutes later. It was Bill, saying that his garage had just blown into the bay.

On the sunporch where Mabel Burghard was sewing, the large window facing the ocean blew in, bringing water and sand with it. George and Carl Dalin rushed to the basement for a door and tried to lash it against the opening of the broken window. The wind was so powerful that it took all the strength they had between the two of them to hold the door in place while they secured it. It was roughly 2:30 when George looked out the window and saw the first wave come over the top of the dunes. It was four feet deep and full of force. Within seconds a second wave followed. This time the wave nearly reached the house, and as it receded it carried away the Burghard bathhouse. "Don't you think it's getting serious?" asked Mabel. Without waiting for a reply, she went upstairs to put on her bathing suit.

All along Long Island, the weather situation was beginning to build. The Lee family's first inkling of trouble in Southampton came when they heard a rhythmic thumping at the door over the sound of Lee's brother's piano-playing. Water from the lake, now risen to a depth equal to the height of Grassmere's porch windows, had carried Dan, a lifeguard and the children's swimming teacher at the Southampton Beach Club, to their door on a log. As he was closing the bathhouse at the beach club, he had been washed off the beach by a wave. Hanging to the log to stay afloat, he was deposited on the family's porch.

* * *

Still, people went down to the beach to watch the waves. Many parents had told their children growing up on Long Island that hurricanes never came to Long Island. A showing of *Typhoon* in the local theater had sparked many questions and discussions on the topic. It was widely accepted that, nor'easters—yes; but hurricanes, with wind speeds up to 155 miles per hour, never came here. The idea of a hurricane didn't cross people's minds even as it was lurking nearby.

Teens who'd been turned away from the movie on Main Street because the theater was flooded and a power line was down across the street decided to go to the beach instead. Several high school seniors looking for a thrill drove out on their lunch break to see the whitecaps and walk on the beach in the high wind. At the corner by the boat basin, they could see a bridge standing on end across the canal and the wind was howling, but they didn't turn back. Others drove down to Rogers Bridge on Beach Lane to see the storm, but when they arrived, the canal and bay had already flooded the road. It was too late to turn back then. They took refuge in the bridge tender's home in one of the bridge towers, where it was agreed that this storm was a particularly nasty nor'easter.[7]

＊ ＊ ＊

In the village of Quogue, as in other town centers back from the waterfront, the severity of the storm became evident much later than it had to those with houses right on the beach. In one store, a man offered a hundred dollars to anyone who would go out and get his dogs out of his beach house. Thomas Fay, twenty-one, and his friend Charles Lucas Jr. jumped at the offer. A hundred dollars was more money than they could afford to pass up, even if they had to split it.

❖ ❖ ❖

Conditions were worsening steadily though less dramatically along the Connecticut coast. Adams Nickerson caught glimpses of the rough water and whitecaps in Long Island Sound as the train moved through Mamaroneck and Rye. The train traveled a mostly coastal route, and Adams began to take the storm seriously when the train crossed into Connecticut. Gazing out the window, he was sure he saw a small pond disappear. The water just seemed to be blown out before his eyes. He turned to see if anyone else on the train had seen it, too, but apparently not. He wondered whether he was the only one who had seen it, if he'd imagined it or if it had happened.

❖ ❖ ❖

In Groton Long Point, Connecticut, north across Long Island and the Sound, the weather still seemed mild and pleasant. Polly Cleaveland was settling into an easy morning with her best friend Fanny Hebert. The two women had made the two-hour drive from Springfield, Massachusetts, several days earlier, ostensibly to shut down the Cleaveland cottage, but the weeklong trip was a much-anticipated annual getaway for both women. No meals to cook, no husbands, and no children. It was heaven, they agreed. This year it seemed even more of a treat because the Cleavelands had rented it out for a month in the summer. The three hundred dollars it fetched would pay the taxes in a year that Harry Cleaveland was feeling pinched. Many of his dental patients, hobbled by the Depression, were still in arrears.

Polly and Fanny would strip the slipcovers from the cushions, take down the calico curtains, and clean the cupboards while they were there, but it was a carefree week away from their home responsibilities that they considered the real luxury. For Polly, it was a chance to talk freely to Fanny about her disappointment over daughter Jean's engagement. Jean, twenty-one, had graduated from secretarial school that spring. Her fiancé was still at Springfield College and had borrowed money to pay for his tuition. Polly had hoped that Jean would marry someone more socially acceptable and established, as had her other daughter, Betty. Betty had married a Harvard graduate. Jean was living at home and working in her father's dental office while his regular secretary was on maternity leave. The atmosphere between mother and daughter had been strained all summer. When Polly got in the car with Fanny and the family Scottie terrier, Bonnie Lassie, she breathed a definite sigh of relief that she was heading off for a few days away. Jean got along best with her father anyhow. Father and daughter were glad to have the house to themselves as they stood in the driveway of the house in Springfield and waved goodbye to Polly.

Polly loved their summerhouse at Groton Long Point Beach. Built in 1936 to their specifications, it was finished in beaverboard throughout. They had built close to the beach, but not on it. They had decided to locate this house on the rear of a beachfront after being bothered by the noise in an earlier house they'd stayed in closer to the beach and boardwalk, where the maids from all the houses along the shore went to sit on the beach stairs and socialize at night.

The maid's room over the garage was an improvement over their old house. Polly had decorated the summer house simply, with curtains and slipcovers in summery blue-and-white ginghams mixed with her favorite big polka dots. Nothing, she was satisfied, was overdone or showy. A lovely antique lamp may have been the only truly valuable furnishing in the house, but the structure itself was roomy and accommodating. Life was comfortable and always casual there, an easy contrast to the more typical formality they observed in Springfield, where Harry Cleaveland was a respected dentist and he and Polly were part of Springfield society. Her daughters had spent every summer in Groton Long Point Beach since they were toddlers. They had loved to play at the beach over at Misquamicut, where the waves were always biggest, but Polly preferred Groton Long Point, which was considered a social notch above Misquamicut. She'd been coming there for sixteen years.

Polly and Fanny had walked the boardwalk in Groton every day they'd been there. Though Polly was known to be opinionated and often unforgiving in her own family, when she was with Fanny, she reverted to her girlish self. The two of them sat for hours and giggled over something that had happened at the Faith Long Church in Springfield where they donated much of their time and energy, or in the ladies' bridge club games that they attended without fail.

This morning the weather looked a bit like rain, and the air was heavy. The sky was a funny color, a few people remarked. A tinge of yellow made it look green. Polly decided to take the day slowly and linger a bit over breakfast. She and Fanny would put the house away in the morning in case the sun came out, and then they could go to the beach in the afternoon. It was almost lunchtime when the milkman knocked on the door. Their breakfast dishes were still in the sink.

"There's quite a blow coming up, Mrs. Cleaveland," he told them. He could see that the women weren't convinced they should react. He explained that houses so close to the water might be going to get wet. He thought they should think about leaving until the storm had passed through. Polly and Fanny mulled it over. They were reluctant to have their plans determined by anyone but themselves, especially the milkman, but perhaps they would err on the side of caution. The sky was getting darker. The milkman added, "I'd be fast about it if I were you" before he moved along to warn the occupants of the next house. He was a neighborhood character and jack-of-all-trades who had collected the garbage and delivered fish and milk to local residents over the years. So Polly and Fanny decided to move to higher ground. First, they would go back to Noank and check out a gift shop that they both liked. They grabbed their pocketbooks and called to Bonnie Lassie, who always jumped gladly into the backseat of the car to go for a ride. Uncharacteristically, they left their unwashed dishes in the sink, and off they went.

Polly and Fanny took the milkman's advice and headed inland for Noank. They felt certain the storm would soon pass. As they'd hoped when they reached the village, their favorite gift shop was open. They went in to browse, and Polly spotted an attractive Victorian footstool. It had a needlepoint cover with a tulip in the center and prettily carved feet. She asked Fanny's opinion. They agreed that it would make a

nice engagement present for Jean, and told the store owner
what Polly was buying it for. Polly and Fanny lingered to
chat with the shopkeeper as they waited for the rain to let
up. Polly paid for the stool with a check. It still had the price
tag tied to its foot when she set it inside the backseat next
to Bonnie Lassie. But the rain showed no sign of lessening,
so they decided to go out for tea in order to kill more time.
Then, despite the rain and lashing wind, they decided to
head back to Groton Long Point. Bonnie Lassie paced the
backseat of the car, whining. She didn't like the sound of
the storm.

❈ ❈ ❈

The tide was half in when Katharine Hepburn and Red
Hammond went down to the water for their celebratory
swim following their game of golf. Despite the breeze, they
were hot after playing golf in such high humidity. Katharine,
who liked winning at everything, was in high spirits. The
wind, the fact that she could lean against it and feel its force
holding her up, was exhilarating. She swam in the water in
front of the house even in the winter and loved the change-
ability of the elements. Sometimes conditions were bracing,
other times they were sublime, but it was the variety that
kept things exciting in her opinion. She and Red jumped and
played in the waves like kids for a while before they got out.
The wind was increasing, and when they climbed out of the
surf and raced for their towels, it had begun to blow sand
that stung as it hit them. Kate realized in the midst of her
high spirits and frolic, as she told Red, "We are in for something special."

Her mother and the cook and her brother were in the house when they got there. They had called in a handyman to nail down the screens on the porch so they wouldn't bang and blow in. He had driven in from Saybrook and parked his car by the side of the house. Suddenly, as they all looked on, his ordinary midsize sedan blew into the nearby lagoon. They were all astonished, but before there was time to say much about it, the laundry wing of the house was ripped away and crashed to the ground. In a flash the windows were blown out or sucked in and two of the brick chimneys blew down. Her brother announced that it was time to leave.

※ ※ ※

In Providence, the wind was blowing and the sky looked more ominous than it had at breakfast, but Lorraine Martin stayed fast in her conviction not to cancel her wedding on account of a little rain. Still, the worsening conditions were beginning to make her nervous.

Things were not better at the home of her groom, Josef Fogel, in the Elmwood section of Providence, where anxiety about the weather was beginning to mount. Marilyn Fogel, the groom's younger sister, watched the trees in the lawn behind their house bending low in the wind. It wasn't raining yet, though, and she thought the brisk wind lent an air of excitement to the morning. It felt like something she'd read about in *Wuthering Heights*. She was ecstatic that her mother had kept her home from high school to get ready for the wedding. There was an air of festivity about the morning that caught her up. Her long semiformal dress and the little silver slippers that matched were already laid out

in her bedroom, and she could hardly wait to wear them.
Her mother read the forecast in the morning paper, "Rain,
heavy at times." She and Marilyn's grandmother started to
fret. It had rained several days during the past week, but
they had hoped the bad weather was over. At least the wedding was indoors, they reassured themselves. The rain was
too bad, sighed her grandmother. Marilyn's father, Josef
Fogel Sr., was becoming impatient with the topic. Young
Josef, who had the most to be anxious about since it was
his wedding day, seemed as calm as ever. "It's going to be
just fine and everyone should relax," her father told them
firmly. He expected the storm, probably a typical nor'easter,
to be cleared up by evening.

In the offices of the *Providence Evening Bulletin* in downtown Providence, war rather than weather was on the mind
of managing editor David Patten. There were threats of war
in Europe and primary elections in the neighboring states
to cover for the paper. Neville Chamberlain, prime minis-
ter of Britain, had returned from Berchtesgaden, where two
days earlier he had submitted to Adolf Hitler's demands of
self-determination for the German-speaking section of the
Sudetenland. This was ominous news for Western Europe.
With a handshake among leaders, the German-speaking
Czechs of Czechoslovakia's border territory were to change
their allegiance to Germany, and all previous treaties vere
considered null. France, once posed to intervene if Germany
invaded Czechoslovakia, uneasily put down her arms. The
Czech leaders threw up their hands in unhappy resignation.
Hitler prepared to move ahead with soldiers, planes, and
tanks. Chamberlain was about to leave for Bad Godesberg,

and some observers at home and abroad were losing confidence in the power of diplomacy to contain Hitler's ambitions. Chamberlain had already given up too much, in the opinion of many who saw his appeasement policy to be an outright betrayal of the Czechs. The Movietone newsreels, updated weekly, that were shown with the previews in the movie theaters downtown were the only images the public had of what was quickly becoming the most dangerous war crisis in Europe since 1914. Newspaper, newsmagazine, and radio accounts of these unfolding world events were critical for keeping the public informed.

Patten made his plans that morning to run the news of the deteriorating situation in Europe prominently on the front page. He considered the Massachusetts and New York City primaries to be big stories and would play them second. In order to stay on top of events as they happened, he stayed at his desk in the newspaper's offices on Fountain Street and followed the news of developments in Europe as they came in on the telegraph wire from Associated Press. He had his own reporters in the field covering the neighboring political races. In addition, there was a little story of the hurricane working up the coast from the Carolinas that he assigned to the inside pages of the paper. He often had such weather stories, but they were seldom more than blips in Providence's rather predictable seasonal weather picture. The storms and weather systems that brewed along the Southern coast didn't come as far north as New England.[8]

VIII

No longer elusive and catlike, GH38 had morphed into a monster as it struck Long Island. With no electricity, phone, or telegraph service, the coastline ahead, across the sound in Connecticut and Rhode Island, could not be alerted. It was three o'clock, and it was too late. No one understood that the storm was continuing to gain speed and strength and that it would grind across Long Island and the Sound in just over an hour to strike the mainland coast at the height of its power. Its deviltry was magnified when it ran into and combined with a frontal system along the Connecticut River Valley and western Massachusetts that would bring between ten and seventeen inches of rainfall over several hours. GH38 was now traveling at 60 miles per hour, the fastest forward-moving speed ever recorded for a hurricane.

At this point, a typical hurricane making landfall would have begun to lose power, but GH38 gained its place in meteorological history by transforming into what meteorolo-

gists call an extratropical storm. When it met the frontal
systems from land, its low pressure center was colder than
the adjoining atmosphere, causing the eye to cool, sink, and
elongate until the cell of the storm spanned a thousand miles,
double the width of a typical hurricane. Now with its own
frontal structure and both tropical maritime and polar con-
tinental air dueling to fuel its speed and strength, GH38
intensified swiftly.

It is unconceivable now to think of a time when a storm
of such magnitude would not have been anticipated with
satellite pictures, those staples of the nightly news during
hurricane season. But they didn't exist. There was no radar.
There was no Weather Channel, no TV reporters in shiny
new foul weather gear standing on beaches shouting warnings over the buffeting gusts. There were no evacuations
ordered, no advisories to batten down the hatches and roll
up the rugs. The element of surprise was as deadly for coastal
New England as the strength of the storm itself.

The strength and power that a mature hurricane packs
is more than even a seasoned meteorologist can wrap his or
her mind around. Every gram of water, a volume about the
size of the tip of a man's thumb, releases 540 calories of
heat as it condenses into water vapor. As the warm tropical air continually rises and recondenses, this huge energy
flow powers a deadly and driving machine that cannot be
stopped. Evaporation cools the mechanism down a bit, but
the impact is negligible. GH38 was five hundred miles across
when it made landfall, and it is mind-boggling to try to quan-
tify its power and strength. Meteorologists now know that
a typical hurricane releases more energy every hour than

an atomic bomb, a comparison that would have been entirely lost in 1938. Author Sebastian Junger in his book *The Perfect Storm,* an account of the 1991 storm of the same name, explained that the combined nuclear arsenals of the United States and Russia do not have enough energy to keep a hurricane running for an entire day. It is the most powerful event on earth, and perhaps the most terrifying to experience, with constant gusting and a sound like fingernails being dragged across a blackboard magnified on a loudspeaker lasting for hours.

Yet the hurricane's blow, as devastating and powerful as it can be, is not its greatest danger. The storm surge that accompanies it is the most terrifying thing; the sea rising out of its shores and engulfing everything in its path like a mythical sea demon. It is a nightmare of nearly biblical proportions and terror. The storm surge is what swept beach strollers and picnickers to their deaths in GH38. It was what caused the high death toll from Hurricane Camille in the southeastern United States in 1969. In Biloxi, Missisippi, where hurricanes occur more frequently and are better understood, revelers took to the beachfront to have hurricane parties and gave no mind to the surge possibilities. When the thunderous twenty-two-foot-high storm surge hit the Louisiana-Mississippi coast, it caused a billion dollars in property losses and washed away 143 lives.

The damage done by a surge can be minimized if it hits at low tide, as did Hurricane Bob, but in 1938 the tide was at its all-time high. It was the peak time of day and also it was the season of the equinox when tides are typically highest as the moon passes closer to the earth than at any other time of year and exerts its strongest gravitational pull, drawing the ocean up onto the shore. The result was that the surge didn't rise and retreat back to the ocean but sustained its grip, holding its victims hostage to the waters for several hours.

The Weather Bureau at this stage had also clearly lost its role as forecaster of the hurricane, though it had issued gale warnings at round noon. People who knew the water, like the Long Island fishermen, were used to hearing the term. It did not imply disaster to them.

The radio forecast George Burghard tuned in that afternoon was made matter-of-factly, with no suggestion of emergency. There was nothing to put people on high alert, to prepare them for the possibility of devastation. There were warnings of "whole gales," and at two o'clock an advisory was released that a tropical storm would be "likely to pass over Long Island and Connecticut late [that] afternoon or early [that] night, attended by shifting gales." People might have worried about a hurricane, but that was a term the forecasters had not used. In fact, at 2:00 P.M. the center of the storm was already east of Lakehurst, New Jersey, and winds had reached hurricane force at Block Island, off the tip of Montauk. Within the next hour, GH38 would make its unexpected arrival at 60 miles per hour on the south shore of Long Island. It was at the height of its strength, spinning at 74 miles per hour around a fifty-mile-wide eye.[9]

In New England, where fewer storms of dangerous proportions threatened, the Weather Bureau was not organized for hurricane work. There were only two weather maps, and forecasts were issued daily, not enough to track

a storm that doubled its forward movement overnight, cost-
ing the Weather Bureau several additional precious hours
of warning. There were four such forecasts per day along
the Gulf Coast, where hurricanes occurred more frequently.

Sweeping in faster than cars could drive, the wildcat
moved across the island and over the Sound. Winds along
its forward and eastern edge, the northeast quadrant, were
moving north. They hit the end of Long Island at Amagansett and Montauk, and would strike the mainland at the Connecticut–Rhode Island border near Westerly and Napatree
Point, where the Moore families and twenty-nine other residents, all oblivious to the coming storm, were targets in
the hurricane's path. When the interior winds were blowing in the same direction as the storm's movement, the
winds on the ground were roughly the sum of the two.
Now they were driving north with gusts over 150 knots
and pushing water before them in a mighty surge.

IX

The prophecy of the old "weather eye" that morning was borne out for Milt Miller. Back in Fort Pond Bay, when the storm hit hard, Milt watched the fish factory just blow apart. First he had to anchor his boss's boats. Captain Edwards had a 110-foot boat, a former WWI subchaser. Then he had his own boat to secure. It was like a bad joke. As soon as he had one tied up, the lines on the other started to break, so he had to tie them over and over again. He had never seen wind or water this rough. The horror of his helplessness dawned on him when the fish factory's steel sheet roof and siding ripped away. The noise was like something he'd never heard before but had imagined in an action comic: overpoweringly loud, violent, and concussive. *Clang! Pow! Bam!* It stayed in your head even after it was over, as though your brain was still vibrating from it. If you let yourself go, you could become hysterical, Milt thought. Eight-by-five-foot pieces of steel soared overhead like kites. There was the terrible temptation to stop and watch; he had never seen anything like this. Yet he knew he was in danger and that the boats were at extreme risk. They were jumping around in the choppy waters like bumblebees, the lines snapping like shoestrings. He knew he should consider his own safety but didn't have time to be truly scared; he and the other half dozen boathands in the boat basin just kept working as hard as they could. He knew Amagansett, Montauk, and Fort Pond Bay were in trouble. He had seen the wind shift south late in the morning. At first it was blowing into Long Island Sound, but the shift caused water to blow in from the bay side. The fish factory was at the lowest spot. He also knew that the *Ocean View,* a boat belonging to the factory, had gone out with twenty men aboard headed up the coast toward Connecticut. He could not get those men out of his mind.

❊ ❊ ❊

Further west along the Long Island coast, the big cat, in its play, had allowed the sun to come out briefly about lunchtime. Tot Greene thought she might be able to get the kids out of the house after all. But it was a false hope. The wind had not dropped, and it felt even more menacing than it had that morning. It was blowing from the northeast then, and Tot thought to herself that the sound reminded her of a woman wailing. Then she heard a loud crash. She was confused about where the sound was coming from until she remembered that she had left the garage doors open. The wind had ripped them off their hinges and hurled them onto the paved driveway. She realized she could not now get the car out of the garage and thought about how to pick up

Norvin at the station. Her mind was racing. At the same time
she noticed there were still linens hanging on the clothes-
line behind the house and she started out to bring them in,
but the force of the wind threw her back against the house.
Moving with all her might, she could not get away. Suddenly
she was scared.

Once she managed to get back into the house, she went
to the phone to call for help, but the line was dead. She
noticed then that the lights were off, too. She walked over
to the sink and turned on the faucet. No water. She was
weighing her options when there was a sound at the front
door and eleven people, including a couple with two babies,
came inside. The group had evacuated an oceanfront house
when the waves had broken through the dunes and started
to flood the interior. Tot reached down into herself and
quelled a growing sense of disorder and panic. She was glad
to see four men in the group, the husband of the cook and
Joseph McFarland and his two sons. The McFarlands had
a moving business and had been on the site moving Tot's
neighbors back to the city. Mr. McFarland had sent his sons
ahead, but as the rising water deepened, he decided it was
time to get out of the house himself. He practically had to
swim to get across the Dune Road to the Greene house and,
to his astonishment, the ocean was still rising. The Greene
house was one hundred yards back from the ocean. Now,
he reported, and Tot had noticed, too, the wind was raging
from the southwest and it had risen high enough that waves
were being propelled against her house. There was hardly
time to think of what to do next except to get above the
water. In stunned disbelief that the waves had crossed Dune

Road and reached this far, they all ran to the second floor. Tot assigned each of the men a child to look after if the house fell in, but they looked at her blankly. None of them could swim. There was only one life preserver.

The sound of breaking glass as the first-floor windows blew in and the cracking sound of window sashes and frames shattering could be heard coming from downstairs. The refrigerator made a loud thud as it fell on its side. But who should get the life preserver? Tot decided that in good conscience it could not be her own child, so she thought she would give it to Otis Bradley, the youngest Bradley child. But Margaret Bradley grabbed it and slipped it on over her head. "Don't you think your little brother, Otis, should have it?" Tot asked. "No, girls first!" was feisty Margaret's response.

By then the ocean was beating through the lower floor and had risen to the height of the second floor, smashing the front staircase as it thrust higher and harder into the house. Everyone climbed into the attic by standing on a folding chair and being boosted from behind, one of the McFarland sons heaving himself up last. There were no lights or windows in the attic, so the men punched a hole in the roof with a crowbar in order to see the bay and have an exit in case the house fell. Suddenly the baby nurse for the two infants began to cry hysterically, saying, "We will all be drowned!" "Shut up!" snapped Tot. Such an outburst to a total stranger was out of character for Tot, but she didn't want the nurse to scare the children. She had no patience for anything but clear thinking now. She began considering options and thinking of features about the house that she had never paid much attention to before. She seemed to recall that the architect had tied the timbers onto a concrete garage floor. There was a concrete front porch on the ocean side and a concrete patio porch on the bay side. Still, she expected the house to go any minute and that everyone would need to float over to the mainland on the roof. The horror of the thought became reality as the group watched a similar roof off a nearby house collapse and slide into the water of Moriches Bay. Then the living room wing and master bedroom above it, portions of the Greene house that had been built on piles, were torn off by waves and floated away.

While huddled with the others on the second floor, Patricia Driver was terrified both for herself and wondering about her parents, who had planned to go fishing after dropping her at the Greene's. When the storm had first worsened, she knew that Mrs. Greene had tried to call all the children's parents to come and get them, but the phone had been dead, so Patricia didn't know where her parents were or if they knew how dire conditions were for her. The sound of banging shutters and the deafening wind terrified her. When the ocean rose over the dunes and headed directly for the house, she had heard a grown-up yell, "Don't let the children see it," but all the children had run to the windows to look, and Patricia, along with the others, had burst into tears. A huge wave, bigger than any they had ever seen before, rose above the dunes and headed right at them, the way one might in a horror movie or nightmare. But Patricia knew that this was for real. The wave came at them over the tops of the dunes and crashed onto the house. Water burst through the windows as they had fled in panic up to the attic. The children cried continually. Sobbing was the only sound Patricia could hear over the noise of the storm itself.

Her parents had gone fishing according to plan. In their twenty-five-foot Jersey sea skiff *Black Duck*, they had started out in the rain, certain that the weather was just a spell of a typical fall storm. They took the boat up near the inlet and caught fish until, at one o'clock, the wind picked up and they decided to head home. They had to stay close to shore with the *Black Duck*, and as they crossed underneath the West Bay bridge, they could hardly see the water beneath them because the foam was so thick and yellowish. It seemed odd to Frank, who assumed the churning water was carrying up sand from the bottom. The tide was low as they came into the Westhampton Beach yacht basin, and as his son Frank tied up the boat, he and Louise worried that the wind would blow him off the bow. No sooner were they back home on Beach Lane than the windows in the house blew out and Frank decided to get everyone out of the house. A small Ford sedan that would hold five people was the only car, so he hurried to get his mother, her guests, his wife Louise, and sons Frank and six-month-old David, eight people, into the car. Frank couldn't drive, so Louise got behind the wheel with David on her lap. They drove off with great guilt and anxiety over leaving John Metcalf, a hired man, Josephine the cook, and Evelyn, the baby nurse behind. They simply told them to leave the house and to get to safety as best they could.

After dropping his mother's guests at the Howell House Hotel, they drove to Riverhead and got the last room available at the Henry Perkins Hotel. Without electricity, candles and flashlights were the only lights. With his family settled,

Frank decided to go back to Westhampton Beach to see if
the help had gotten out and what he might be able to do in
the house, but he could get no further than Main Street. His
mind was racing: Where was Patricia? The Greene's house
was five miles west of the West Bay bridge, the last house
on the bay side before Moriches Inlet. He and Louise were
worried sick.

❊ ❊ ❊

The Great Hurricane was pummeling the Hamptons hard
by three o'clock. The Burghard house, also substantially
built with a concrete floor under the lower level, which
housed the servants and garage, was now flooded with three
feet of water. Burghard believed this was probably the worst
the storm would be. He suggested to Carl Dalin that he
should go down and get some clothing for himself and his
wife Selma so they could stay upstairs in the third-floor guest
room that night. Then he went around to the west side of
the cottage, which was in the lee side of the wind, to take
down some of his antennas, but as he stepped out from the
basement another big wave washed over the dunes and he
had to grab onto one of the antenna poles to keep from
being washed away. He looked up to see John Avery, the
coastguardsman on duty in the nearby watchtower, wading toward him in the churning surf. Avery was shouting.
He told Burghard to get his wife and the servants out of
the cottage and try to make it to the mainland. It was 3:30.
Both men knew high tide was still to come, at about six
o'clock. George couldn't imagine how much worse it could
get.

On the south side of Long Island the barometer was already reading 27.94, the lowest it would go. The moment of the storm's ferocious landfall had arrived.

Their house faced the ocean and was backed by the bay. It was a half mile east to reach a bridge that they could cross to the mainland. George worried about the condition of the bridge, but he knew it was their best chance. Anyhow, if they couldn't cross the bridge, the bay was narrow at that point, only about a hundred feet to the mainland, and he and Mabel could swim it. For contrast, the bay was almost a mile wide to the mainland from their house. It was worth a try. He went inside and told Carl and Selma to get ready to leave and gave Carl a pair of boots. Mabel went upstairs to put on shoes. They were worried about walking through so much wreckage. Mabel, game as usual, put on sandals, slung a handbag on her arm, then took her lorgnettes and put them around her neck. George looked around his third-floor bedroom. The surf, bubbling and white, was rushing through the bottom of the house. He quickly looked at his watch and cuff links and keys and decided to leave them, but on impulse he grabbed the season tickets for tennis matches at Forest Hills and put them in his pants pocket. He still had hopes of seeing the semifinals on Thursday.

The Dalins, both in their sixties, were reluctant to leave. Mrs. Dalin was still working in the kitchen. Carl Dalin wanted to take his car, a new car Burghard had given him earlier in the summer that he was especially proud of. Burghard began to explain that the situation was more serious than that. Mabel came downstairs and put on a leather jacket, one she had bought in Hawaii and loved, over her swimsuit. She decided she and George would carry their two dogs, Peter the cocker spaniel, and Bitzie the wirehaired fox terrier.

The only exit from the house now was from the garage. Waist-high foaming water churned against the door and kept George from opening it. With the help of Coastguardsman Avery, who had stayed on hand to prevail upon the Dalins to leave, he finally managed to shove it out and jam it open as water poured in.

George and Mabel, with their dogs, stepped into the waves and started out. Avery told them to begin on foot for the bridge that would take them inland over Moriches Bay. The Dalins hung back, still questioning whether it was absolutely necessary to go. Avery stayed behind with the older couple to make sure that they would leave the house.

Mrs. Dalin, who told him she couldn't swim, was terrified. Avery put an arm around her and dragged her to the hedge where the Burghards had regrouped and were waiting. Mabel tried to be reassuring and told her to grab onto a telegraph pole. They looked back to see Carl Dalin finally leave the driveway only to reach a fence post along the road and sit down. The others called to him. They thought that since he was downwind from them, the wind would carry their voices, but he didn't budge. He just kept looking down at the water.

The wind had so far been blowing east, but now it shifted to from the south and blew right in from the ocean and over the dunes. Fifty-foot waves, green and monolithic, roared onto shore and broke on top of everything in their path: houses, dunes, roads, people. The Burghards held tight to the telephone poles to keep from washing away, but the real hazard now was the wreckage being hurled by the sea with a force that turned the smallest log, fence post, bureau drawer, or chair into a deadly weapon. Mabel was submerged by the waves several times, but she managed to surface, and the dogs had stayed on top of the hedge. Mrs. Dalin became hysterical and dragged the others to a pole closer to her husband, though he still sat in a frozen pose, unmoving.

Now it looked impossible to walk east toward the bridge. Even if they could withstand the wind and waves, the visibility was terrible. They could hardly make out the land from the water, and the sky was dark and full of blowing sand. Avery, George, and Mabel decided that their only chance at surviving would be to swim north across the mile-wide bay to the mainland. The men took off their coats and boots and cut off their trouser legs with a penknife. Mabel let her precious leather jacket go, but she hung onto her purse and kept her lorgnette hanging around her neck. George spotted a small rowboat tied to their neighbors' dock and he ran for it, hoping that he could put the Dalins in it, but the moment he got close enough to reach for it, the line that held it snapped and the boat raced away in the wind. He watched the Coast Guard station with its steel tower and one-hundred-foot radio mast fall over like a Tinkertoy model and wash into the bay. It all seemed to happen silently; the only constant was the high-pitched sound of the hurricane that overrode all other sound. George now worried that the power lines on Dune Road would come down and electrocute them in the water. He had forgotten that the power was out.

The only alternative now seemed to be to go to the visibly weakening neighbor's dock and lie flat on it, hoping that, if the waves should wash the dock away, they would be safely on it. They called to the Dalins, but Mrs. Dalin held to her phone pole with a death grip and her husband had not looked up from his place by the fence post. The Burghards put their dogs on the hedge. They knew they had to leave them, but Peter, the cocker spaniel, looked so woebegone that George tucked him under his arm. He supported Mabel with the other one. As they reached the dock, they saw that Bitzie, the fox terrier, was swimming alongside. Their assumption was that the storm had peaked, would surely be ending, and that they would come back soon by boat to pick up the dogs and the Dalins. Waiting for the dock to wash out, Mabel watched the bathhouse of their neighbor's cottage break up. When it did, she grabbed a piece of it and took the two dogs with her. George and Avery climbed on and waited for the next high wave to carry them and their raft into the bay. They were not disappointed. For a time it seemed to them that the wind was blowing water out of the bay. Each wave that propelled the Burghards and their raft inland dropped them onto the muddy bottom of the bay to await the next lift from the surf behind them. It was terrifying to wait, wondering if that incoming wave would crush or carry them along. By this time, fuel tanks, planks, and a limitless list of debris nearly covered the surface of the water. Doors and boards flew above their heads in a tempest that had begun to feel like the apocalypse. They could not see another person. Rescue was out of the question. It was as though they were the last people on earth, washing to an unknown future.

The wind was increasing, and with it came semidarkness and the helpless feeling of being lifted along and then dropped into the trough of the waves. Mabel washed off the raft after one large wave hit them and managed to get back aboard by grabbing onto her husband's foot. Bitzie climbed up the back of Mabel's neck to keep from drowning in water that was now rising. The men grabbed a piece of wood that could serve as a raft for the dogs and put them aboard, but once the pets floated a hundred feet ahead of their owners, they both jumped off and swam back. The wind was now blowing at 100 miles per hour. It was close to five o'clock.

Floating on the water, the Burghards soon lost all sense of reality. Their raft was repeatedly submerged and they were washed off by every breaker from the sea. When they could exert any control over the raft, they tried to dodge the debris in the water that posed the chief obstacle to their safety. Halves of houses roared by, roofs rushed by like motorboats. Cars floated in the surf until the wind got behind them and threw them up into the air like breaching whales. Mabel believed she saw a motorboat speeding by and hoped it was going back after the Dalins. But it was just an illusion created by the corner of a house that was grounded. The wind and moving water made it look as if it were moving. There were moments of total amazement at what they were seeing and other times of cringing fear, but there was little they could do but hang on and ride it out. Fortunately, as the storm moved over them, the wind had shifted to the south and was blowing them into the bay back to Oneck Point and not out to sea. George recognized signs that they were in the main channel. He knew they were a mile from land, and that the water was deeper in the channel. Their raft was starting to sink. A piece of a house, studded with nails where it had been ripped apart, floated by and John Avery and George Burghard grabbed hold of it. With Mabel and the two dogs, they transferred over to it and could sit above the water and even brace their feet.

When they were three hundred feet off of Oneck Point, they sighted people onshore, the first time they had seen other human beings since their ordeal began. Rather than relief, they felt apprehension that as they reached shore they would be crushed by wreckage. The surface of the water was thick with it. The waves were still getting higher and higher. At one point a plank was carried by a wave onto their makeshift raft right between George and Mabel. George was occupied pushing a roof off one side while Mabel tried to guide the plank with her hands and sprained her wrist in the process. At last the wind and the waves carried them into a clump of berry bushes fifty feet from the porch of the house where they had spotted the people. No one was in sight to lend a hand by the time they washed ashore. Feeling a bit like automatons, they trudged along through three feet of water to the Westhampton golf course and up the fairway to the eleventh hole, where it was dry. A woman stepped out onto a porch that had been empty before and waded over to them. She was hysterical and spoke nonsensically, which became understandable when they learned she was stranded with two babies in the house. John Avery went to help her carry them. George and Mabel continued walking up the golf course. It had stopped raining and the sun even poked through. Mabel was wearing only her swimsuit, but she had her purse worn over her arm. It had left welts where the handle had dug into her. Both had cuts, bruises, and scratches, and Mabel's wrist had begun to swell, but around her neck like a badge hung her lorgnettes.

They walked two more miles before they recognized where they were and saw a house they knew. George went in with the intention of using the telephone, but of course, there was no phone service left in the area. He was disoriented by a dip in the road, which he knew to be a mile from Westhampton Beach, but he had never seen water there before. Now the dip was a roaring torrent one hundred feet wide with a waterfall to one side. Wreckage was pouring through like cars on an amusement park ride. They watched a telephone truck try to cross the submerged section of road and stall.

The wind was now chilling them to the bone, and they looked to anyone passing by for assistance, but the one car that drove up didn't acknowledge them and went on. A woman came out of a house and looked right through them, which was the moment they realized that the whole community had suffered a disaster of such magnitude that their own narrow escape was just one of many horror stories. People were taxed to the limit and could think only of their own survival. Finally, a man seeking directions from them to Westhampton stopped his car. They asked for a ride and he dropped them off at Perry's drugstore in the town, which was emptied of people. Six feet of water was standing in the street and still rising. The wind picked up and it began to rain again. In the emptied streets, they had a feeling of complete desolation.

Finally a man leading an old lady walked by and George called to him, "Where can we get warm?" He led them to the Howell House, which had a stove. The hotel had closed for the season that morning but opened its doors to people in the storm. George told the other survivors that he and Mabel had just swum across the bay, but they just looked away. Some were worried with the water still rising that this was the end of Long Island. Finally someone brought them coffee and brandy to warm them up. The hotel staff was made up wholly of black men and women, who prayed and chanted while the water was still rising. Then around six o'clock, as though their prayers had been answered, the water, risen by then to eight feet on Main Street, started to recede. George asked the hotel manager to allow him up to the third floor where he could look across to the dunes toward home. It was dusk, but there was still enough light to see that there wasn't a house standing. There wasn't any sign of the Dalins, either. There wouldn't be.

※ ※ ※

When Capt. Dan Grimshaw decided to turn his boat *Robert E.* around and head back for Fort Pond Bay, he got on his ship-to-shore radio to learn if there were any weather warnings. "Gale-force winds" was the only prediction he heard, and to the professional fishermen of Long Island, the 32 to 63 mile per hour winds that "gale-force" suggested were a nuisance and a real storm to contend with, but they weren't anything to be scared of. The forecasters were going to be of no use, he could see. The wind, he figured, was already blowing 90 miles an hour. It was a barometer reading of 28.10 inches that convinced him to get out of the Sound, get the boat safely moored, get his men squared away, and get ashore. He made fast to the first unoccupied mooring he saw. It wasn't his mooring, but he knew that its owner was away. He asked deckhand Stevie Dellapolla to row him in to the dock in the dinghy and then row back on his own, to stay onboard with the two other men, and watch the boat. In Stevie's estimation the other two crewmen were cheap help, guys who were still learning. Even though at eighteen he was younger than they were, he'd been working on boats since he was fourteen and knew the *Robert E.* He knew Captain Dan was putting important trust in him He was anxious to put the captain ashore and get back to the boat, where he would be top crewman.

The wind was picking up fast. As Stevie rowed back out toward the *Robert E.*, the gusts felt as if they were twice as strong as when he'd started ashore with Captain Dan. When he was within two hundred feet of the boat, the dinghy rode up on a high wave and the wind got under the bow, flipping it. Stevie did not know how to swim. He thrashed wildly toward the dinghy, which was blowing across the surface of the water, and just managed to get a handhold. Then, tiring fast, he heaved himself on top of the overturned craft and looked around. Before he had time to get his bearings, he was washed off. This time he didn't have the strength to kick and thrash to get back on. In an eerie moment of calm, he prepared himself to drown. The next moment he saw a piece of half-inch rope, so near to his hand that it seemed to almost be sliding through his palm. He grabbed it, certain that it had come to him as a divine act.

If so, God was working through his fellow crewmen

on the *Robert E.* They had watched his debacle, and when he was washed off the dinghy the second time, they ran to the bow and threw the swordfish keg with its six-hundred-foot-long line to him. As he held on tightly, reenergized now by what he felt certain was God's decision to save his life, the crewmen pulled him in.

When his two shipmates hauled Stevie Dellapolla aboard with the swordfish keg, they had to pry his fingers off of the rope. "You can let go now," one of the men teased him, trying to get him to loosen his grip. Stevie went belowdecks to lie down. The men piled blankets on top of him to try to get his body temperature back to normal. He drifted in and out of sleep with exhaustion. It was almost an hour later when he heard shouts that the boat had broken its mooring line. Stevie ran up on deck and the three men watched, helplessly, as the boat was whisked up the harbor toward Culloden Point and the lighthouse. They understood that if they cleared the point, they would be washed out to sea. The three men had spread out on the boat and each stood roughly fifty feet from the other man. Not a word was exchanged as each watched anxiously to learn his fate. The wind was blowing about 100 miles per hour, and the deckhands couldn't be heard even when they screamed. Stevie thought, standing midships, that it was like being alone with God. He figured each of them had accepted death as a reality by now. He had. Then the wind shifted and, rather than heading out to sea, the boat was being blown toward shore, as though Neptune or a different capricious sea god had changed his mind about their fate. Stevie felt a heightened sense of awareness. Everything felt strange to him, the wind, his precarious hold on life, his distance from the other men, just everything. There is a God, he thought. He had seen evidence. A half-inch-thick length of rope.

When the boat came ashore, he was standing on the rail. He knew that at a depth of six to eight feet the vessel would strike the bottom, but to jump off too soon meant risking that it would be blown on top of him. Each man had to gauge his own best moment to leap. Stevie was in the middle, his companions at the stern and the bow. He jumped first, and they all made it to shore.

It hardly felt less dangerous or disastrous ashore except that the threat of drowning wasn't imminent. It was pouring rain and the three men were soaked and chilled. The sky was dark with wind and rain. They knew they were in a section called The Meadows, where a few houses were located amid the dunes and sea grass. The first house they reached was occupied by three women who came to the door, aghast at the appearance, like drowned rats, of their callers. The women offered them food to eat, but the men asked for dry clothing. Apologetically and with a few smiles, the women offered what they had. It was all women's clothing. The fishermen put on the women's cotton panties and flowered dresses before they set out to walk toward the railroad station a mile and a half beyond. A mile down the road a trucker stopped to pick them up. The men had almost forgotten how ridiculous they looked until they saw the look on the driver's face as they scrambled into the truck, their blue-and-white flowered skirts whipping around them. They had a good laugh, but the fishermen were almost too tired for mirth. The driver, a man they recognized, told them they couldn't get west to Amagansett, where they were from, because the ocean had broken through at Napeague, so he took them to the only place they could reach, Montauk. The Montauk Manor Hotel, which had been closing for the season, had opened its doors to refugees from the storm, of which there were now close to a hundred.

Around Fort Pond, the eastern end of Long Island is only a half mile wide from north to south. The flat beach on the south side, unlike the dunes farther west in the Hamptons, met the road and quickly became a swamp further inland. There were no bushes or trees, only grass and cattle grazing. When the wind and water started blowing in from the ocean, there was no place to go. The 90 to 100 mile per hour winds made the Fort Pond, typically a quiet refuge for fishermen and sailors, as treacherous as the sea. It had begun to look as if the ocean would rise from the south across the sand and grass and meet it, that a flood of biblical proportions was coming to engulf them. In the sparse vegetation and flat land there was no place to hide. Nearly all the houses were flimsily built and close enough to the water so that the fishermen could see their own boats tied to stakes. This part of the island was hit by the northeastern arc of the oncoming storm, known to sailors as the most dangerous quadrant of any hurricane, where the speed of the winds was added to the velocity of the storm itself. Eastern Long Island was a mere speck on its path. Most fishermen knew that high tide was yet to come within the next two hours. It would reach its annual high because of the autumnal equinox. Across those barrens, survivors scrambled toward Montauk—toward any refuge—but winds gusted over 180 miles per hour and waves between thirty and fifty feet high were pounding the coastline, emphasizing the impression that the end of the world had come.

❄ ❄ ❄

Helen Bengtson settled in among the dozen people who had
been led into the Duryea house by Perry Duryea's brother-
in-law Stuart. He didn't want people tracking water onto
the nicely varnished sunroom floor, so he asked them to
spread around newspapers before they sat down. The men
who had come in off the water were soaking wet and given
some of Mary Duryea's—not Perry's—clothes, Helen noted
with some amusement, to put on. Shivering, they wrapped
themselves tightly in the coats and dressing gowns. The mot-
ley group huddled together uneasily in the living room and
sunroom as the hurricane raged outside. The wind sounded
like a screaming demon, but it lulled Helen, phlegmatic as
usual, to sleep.

❄ ❄ ❄

Perry Duryea had no idea that the weather conditions at
Fort Pond had driven his staff into his home, but he was
worried enough about his lobster business and the dock on
Fort Pond that he decided to turn back for Long Island even
as he approached New York City. Headed east, he made
the best time he could, but in the wind and rain it was increasingly evident that the storm was serious. He took his
wife to her sister's place in East Hampton to keep her out
of harm's way and made the last leg of the trip to Montauk
on his own. By the time he got to Napeague, the low spot
between Amagansett and Montauk, the water was four to
five feet deep on the road ahead. It was useless trying to call,
and it was already dark. He'd heard rumors that people had

been killed. Power and phone lines were out everywhere. He had never seen a storm like this one. He had no idea what he would find when — and if — he got to the other side, but he was determined to get there. He appropriated a tractor to have ready to make the crossing as soon as the water was low enough.

* * *

Helen Bengtson, awake now, huddled with the others in the Duryea house. She was worried about her mother, father, and younger brother. As time went on and the storm showed no signs of abating, nerves grew increasingly frayed among those in the Duryea living room and on the sunporch. There was no way to get in touch with anyone, to know what was happening. She also had a random thought: she'd left a brand-new Underwood typewriter on the floor of her bedroom.

Her father had returned home from moving his boats to safety to discover that the water had risen four feet into his own house. He tried to put his wife and son in the car and drive away, but the water had already flooded the engine, so he put three-year-old Leslie on his shoulders and took his wife, trembling with fear because she did not know how to swim, by the hand. Together they walked a quarter mile to the train tracks, just high enough to be clear of the water. The conductor, who had been running behind schedule in the storm, had begun heading west back toward New York City, but when he realized that the residents in low places adjacent to the tracks were trapped and the water was still rising, he reversed direction and began backing up the track to Montauk, through low scrub pines and oaks, then across those flat windswept fields, at a pace slow enough to allow people to jump aboard. Helen's family made it onto the train.

The train backed up all the way to Montauk, where the refugees were taken into the Montauk Manor. The owners had closed it for the season the previous Monday and the beds were already stripped, but they threw open their doors and took in anyone who needed a place to sleep. The Bengtson family was already there when Stevie Dellapolla and his shipmates made their entrance, a vision in their flowery dresses.

※ ※ ※

In the attic of the Greene house, everyone was miserable and cold. They were also relieved that they had not had to plunge out of the hole that the men had knocked through the roof. The hurricane seemed to be over when the group decided to make its way to a concrete-and-stone house on the other side of Dune Road. Tot did not like the idea of invading a friend's house, but she was no longer in charge of a group that had developed a character of its own. When they arrived, the men broke in the glass door to gain entry and build a fire in the fireplace. Tot protested loudly when they took the drawers of Mrs. Jones's antique tables and dressers to burn. After that she seemed to give up. They were all cold and damp in their summer clothes, and the children were shivering uncontrollably. Tot took them upstairs and put them to bed, pulling down the draperies to wrap around them. Patricia, the oldest, tried to keep the others quiet. All five children were put in one bed to keep warm, swaddled up like sausages. The wind was still blowing and Patricia thought she could hear the other children's hearts beating, they were still so afraid. One boy stood up and vomited, whether it was out of fear or from the bread with ketchup and condensed milk that Mrs. Greene had fed them, they couldn't be certain. Patricia tried to muffle her own cries as she thought about her family. She remembers now that the wind outside was like the gust that carried the Wicked Witch in *The Wizard of Oz* furiously aloft on her bicycle.

Tot had done her best to get the children to safety and comfort them. She, too, was exhausted. She had been so busy dealing moment to moment with each new crisis and decision as they arose that she had hardly had time to think of her husband Norvin. Surely he had heard about the hurricane by now. Typically, he would be traveling out to Westhampton from the city at this hour, but she had no idea what had happened to the trains or the other areas of Long Island for that matter. She knew he would be worried since their house sat so close to the water. Now she could do nothing but worry and wait herself.

❊ ❊ ❊

Norvin worked as a stockbroker in New York City and made it his practice during the summer to come out to Westhampton on Wednesday after work. Like most people working in New York City that day, he had no idea the extent to which the storm was to terrorize the residents of Long Island. Wind and rain had taken over for much of the day in New York City, including when he boarded the train to take him to the Hamptons. The first sign of trouble came at Manorville, where the train was stopped because of fallen trees on the track. The time it took for the crew to clear the tracks with axes and saws put the train behind schedule. Norvin was sorry that Tot would likely have to wait for him in Westhampton. When the train pulled into Speonk, a station roughly seven miles from the beach, the signs were more ominous. The conductor announced that they could get no further because a train was off the track in Westhampton. Norvin wanted to phone Tot, but the phones were out. He and a few other passengers who were also headed toward Westhampton Beach decided to hire a car to take them the rest of the way, but once they were on the road, a big fallen tree blocked the way. They decided to walk until an acquaintance pulled up and offered them a ride. One rider asked the driver to take him to his Dune house and then to take Norvin Greene to his home on Dune Road. "There are no dunes," the man replied. "They have disappeared." Instead, he volunteered to take them to the Patio emergency police station. Now full of dread, they rode to the makeshift station inside the Patio Restaurant. With the power out, a candle was used to read the names of survivors off a yellow pad. Norvin read as fast as he could. The names of his wife and children were not on the list. Then he overheard a local gas station owner remark ". . . and that lovely Mrs. Greene with her two children, all washed out to sea!"

"How do you know?" asked Norvin.

The man said he didn't really know anything for sure, except that the dunes were gone. He suggested they go to the country club, which had been set up as a mortuary, to look for bodies. Something turned in the pit of Norvin's stomach. He wanted more information. He wasn't ready yet to go looking for bodies. It was between five and six o'clock.

He joined forces with Ned Lea, another man who was looking for his wife, and the two of them jumped into Ned's Packard two-seater and headed to Riverhead, where they'd heard some survivors had been taken. Neither Norvin's family nor Ned's wife were listed as being there. Norvin realized he was almost faint from hunger. He ordered a roast beef sandwich, which was all the two men had to eat the rest of the night.

Otis Bradley, father of Margaret and Otis Jr., who had been guests of the Greene children that afternoon, had heard about the hurricane in New York by now and hurried out to Westhampton by taxi. When he saw Norvin, he asked the Coast Guard to take the two of them to the dunes that were still standing, but the coastguardsmen refused. Conditions were still too dangerous, they said. Sunken autos and debris from all the houses that had blown into the bay made navigation impossible. They found a friend who had a boat in a nearby boathouse, and they decided to take it out to try and assess the damage. As they were trying to get the boat out, the door chains to the boathouse door broke and it fell onto the car, smashing the windshield. The men had to enlist more help to lift the door, which meant returning to the village. They would have to wait now until morning light to go out to the dunes.

Up in Connecticut, beyond the full fury of the oncoming storm, Emily Fowler was wondering how she and Atwood Ely could have been so foolish as to set out sailing in such a gale. It was past midday, and they had been on the water less than an hour when conditions started to get rough. The two of them together couldn't keep the boat flat on the water even when they trimmed the sail and hiked out on the windward rail. In the inimitable tradition of sailboats, when one thing, however small, goes wrong, another problem is sure to follow. Emily and Atwood were trying to fix a problem with the tiller when the sail dropped down from the top of the mast. The boat was swept along by the wind in the flapping sail, completely beyond their control. Suddenly they were both out of the boat and in the water. Atwood lost his grip and swam off, shouting to be heard over the wind that he was going to get help. "I'll swim ashore and get the launch to come get you," he cried.

Emily was a good swimmer and fearless about water, but she had no idea where she was. It began to rain hard. Visibility was poor, and in the astonishingly high wind she could not make out whether she was still in the Connecticut River or if she were being blown past the point and out to the open sea. There was nothing to do but hang tight to the boat and go with it, until she lost hold of the gunwale in a gust. The rough water seemed to yank it right out of her grasp. She grabbed on to a passing piece of wood that looked to her like firewood, but it was enough to keep her afloat. The wind and current drove her close enough to shore to see cows on land. With a sense of some relief, she thought she knew where she was, near the point at the mouth of the river. At least she had not blown out to sea. At the mouth of the river was a place called Black Hall on the easternmost point, where a squatters' colony had sprung up during the Depression. The wind was blowing Emily and her log in close enough that she could almost reach the flimsy makeshift houses, now under several feet of water. She was too disoriented to know for certain, but she thought the wind had shifted. It was like a dream, she was flying by on the water so fast. Finally she managed in passing to grab at a post that supported a front porch overhang. She hoped she would be able to pull herself over to the shack and climb out of the water, but when she tugged on it, the post came with her instead. The water was shallow enough that the post touched bottom, so she struggled to pole her way toward land with it. Her feet touched bottom just as a sudden surge of water sent her spinning, and she was afloat all over again. She was amazed at how suddenly the water came, like something in the story of Noah and the ark. The house where she had grabbed the post was almost completely covered with water. Some of the adjacent marshes were being flooded, and Emily watched as cows and horses began swimming, lifted out to sea. If she were caught in the water with them, she thought, any terrified floating animal would try to climb up on her and she would drown. The wool swimsuit under her shorts and shirt was completely soaked, and she was cold and shivering. At last the water was shallow enough so she could drag herself ashore. She had been afloat more than two hours.

* * *

It was 3:30 when The Bostonian train carrying Adams Nickerson toward Boston and Framingham, Massachusetts, ran afoul of the weather. Conditions looked ominous when the train pulled out of New London. Blown-down trees littered the tracks as it approached Stonington, Connecticut, and water was pounding both sides of the causeway beneath the rails. The train trembled in the wind.

In Stonington, the windows of the signal tower had been blown out, and water had risen from Block Island Sound in the south over the narrow stretch of land that separated the tracks from the water. The engineer received word by radio that a forty-foot schooner was on the trestle ahead. He climbed down from the engine and walked a thousand feet between the train and the tower to find out about the conditions, but before he could get back to the train, a surge of water waist-high rushed over the tracks. The tracks under the rear cars had already started to give way, and the passengers and crew, figuring the engine was the heaviest and least likely to topple over, began moving toward the front. Some passengers panicked and jumped into the water, now rising rapidly, hoping to swim to higher ground.

Adams did not want to jump and get his new brown wool suit wet, so he left his tennis racket and camera on his seat and started moving through the cars toward the front. In every car he and his fellow passengers tried to gauge how much the car was swaying. Order was quickly breaking down. In one car, Adams noticed a woman beating the windows with her fist, even though there were exits at both ends of the train. In another car, filled mostly with prep school kids, no one would take the conductor seriously when he told them to move to the cars in front. The water was now so high that boats from the Sound and surrounding bays were being blown inland over the tracks. Several slammed against the train.

Out of patience with the unruly schoolboys, Conductor Richards ripped open his emergency case and pulled out the fire ax. He threatened them with it if they didn't get moving. They got up and moved to the car behind the baggage car. The water was shoulder-high at this point and, despite the crew's admonition to stay in the train and move forward, some passengers leapt from windows, doors, and platforms The steward had kept the dining car in operation to assuage the anxiety of the passengers, but the moment came when it too had to be evacuated. Some passengers objected to leaving because they hadn't yet finished meals they had paid for until the conductor told them, "Get out or I'll throw you out." The dining steward was more amused when the gruff conductor stormed at him, "Get that little Irish ass of yours out of here!" His sense of humor soon turned to fear when he noticed that the car had already started to tilt to the left.[10]

The brakes locked into their emergency mode when a timber washed into them hard. The wind was now 120 miles an hour, and a number of storm-driven vessels, including the schooner the engineer had been warned about, were driven into the train's path.

Women and children had been herded into the locomotive, with the rest of the passengers crowded into the front car. The conductor and engineer began working frantically to get the train moving so they could reach higher ground. At the rate the water was rising, it looked like five minutes was about all they had to make it. Air was escaping from a hose that had been hit by an obstruction, so the crew turned off the air in hopes of building up enough pressure to get the train moving. One crewman heroically volunteered that, because he was younger than Conductor Richards, he would jump into the water to make the needed repairs.

Water was up to his chin and he had to work with his head beneath the waves to turn off the air and pull the pin that connected the locomotive engine and first car from the other six cars. He emerged at the rear platform looking half drowned, but the job was done. The engine and its lone car moved to safety.

Adams was one of the eighty or so passengers who got off the train. He had moved early enough to the front car so that he was able to step onto dry land before the water rose any further and before the largest vessel, a schooner, slammed into the train.

He and the other passengers who had made it off The Bostonian train were guided to Stonington. He did not realize how lucky he had been. The trestle the train was sitting on had completely washed away in the torrent only minutes after the engine and car had moved across to higher ground and the remaining passengers had been evacuated. Several people died trying to make it to safety from cars that were stopped on the tracks over Stonington Harbor. When one woman was swept into the harbor from the tracks, a porter, Chester Walker, jumped in to save her, but both drowned in the raging water below.

Some of the older St. Marks boys who had jumped into the water and struck out on their own reached a wedding party outside the town. They were offered champagne and hors d'oeuvres and a place to rest and keep dry in the home of the bride. But Adams, fourteen, was herded with other train passengers to the town hall to sleep on a bench. A man seated next to him told how, as he had made his way off the derailed train, he had spied a doll floating past in the water.

When he picked it up, it was a baby, whose life he had saved. He kept Adams awake by telling the story over and over again. Adams' frustration was somewhat assuaged when he was offered his first cup of coffee. He'd never had coffee before. It was one of the things about the day he would always remember. That, and that he had kept his new suit dry.

* * *

Five miles east along the coast was the southwestern tip of mainland Rhode Island, Napatree Point, where the members of the Mother's Club from Westerly, Rhode Island's Christ Episcopal Church were gathered for lunch. They were pleased with how the day had gone when Reverend Tobin left following their picnic. They had attended their special mass at 10:00 and then driven seven miles to Mae Lowry's cottage, which sat on the inland side of the road that ran along the ocean. Quanicontag Pond sat behind. Mae had skipped mass to prepare the lunch. Reverend Tobin would have liked to linger, but he had to return to officiate at a funeral at two and agreed to drive Ellie Livingston's four-year-old grandson, who was frightened by the high waves, back to town. They had watched a linestorm along the beach from the Lowry house, but they weren't alarmed. Their neighbors on the ocean side were more unsettled by the wind and high surf, and as they packed the car to leave, they asked the Lowry party of women if anyone would like a ride back to town. Mae and her guests declined; they rather liked the storm, they said. There was excitement in the way it drove their dresses tight to the sides of their bodies, blew their hair, and made them feel liberated, even a little wild.

You could do nothing in such conditions but just submit—and be blown to bits. But they thought they would like to watch the storm on the water from the Wells's cottage, which was both more substantial and on the waterfront, so they moved to the house across the road. It wasn't long before it was too windy to be out on the porch, so they decided to go inside and watch it from there.

There still was not much to see. Except for the wind and rain that typically accompanied a nor'easter in the area, the weather seemed deceptively routine. There was no hint that the hurricane, the big cat, was polishing itself off Long Island and about to pounce on the mainland.

X

Further along Napatree Point on the ocean side of Fort Road that ran its length, a brisk morning wind inspired Cathy Moore's mother Catherine to tackle the laundry even though she had less help than she was accustomed to in summer. With ten people in the house, the dirty laundry had begun to pile up. Catherine and her two maids had to double-pin the wet pinafores, knickerbockers, sailor dresses, and aprons on the line to keep them from blowing away.

Catherine headed inside to ask her twelve-year-old son Geoffrey and the young hired man Andy, twenty-three, to bail out the family boats that were full of water from rain the day before. The boys went to work, and by eleven o'clock they were finished. But no sooner had they returned to the house than Andy saw through the window that the dinghy, ten-year-old Anne's sailboat, had come off its mooring line and was drifting across the harbor toward Sandy Point. Geoffrey and Andy ran down to the small dock in front of

the house, and their mother watched them jump in the rowboat to go after it. The boys pulled as hard as they could,
but their boat didn't appear to be moving. The dinghy was
moving too fast, and Catherine felt certain they would never
be able to catch it, let alone row back against such a stiff
breeze. Watching them get farther and farther away, Catherine became alarmed and ran to the phone to call the Coast
Guard station for help. From her window she watched the
Coast Guard head out, but by then Geoffrey's boat was just
barely visible.

She waited anxiously until the Coast Guard called an
hour later to say that they had not seen either the dinghy or
Geoffrey's boat.

"I'll go out myself if one of your guards will come with
me," she told the captain, offering up the family's cabin
cruiser.

The Coast Guard declined her offer, but promised to
go out again. Catherine grew worried enough to call her
husband Jeff and ask him to come down from his office in
Westerly. It was always the same with boats and water, they
knew. Safety and calm could change to chaos in an instant.

Jeff was having his own small drama in his office at
the George C. Moore Factory that morning in Westerly.
He'd had a pain in his chest and arm that seemed to be symp-
toms of a mild heart attack, but he refused to take them
seriously. A former high school and college football player,
he was a strong man who still saw himself as something of
an athlete, in prime health and invincible at forty, even
though he didn't play ball or exercise much anymore, except for boating. When Catherine phoned, he certainly felt

well enough to drive down to Napatree, and he was concerned by her report of the conditions and the idea of the
boys struggling to get the dinghy back.

As the wind began to howl through the house, Catherine
scanned the shoreline of Sandy Point with binoculars until
she spotted two figures she thought could be Geoffrey and
Andy. It appeared that she could reach them by road, so she
decided to go after them herself in the smaller of the family's
two cars. It was low tide, and she hoped the car could make
it on the sand. But the wind had already blown the waves up
over the road in that direction, so she had to turn back.
When she reached the house, she saw Jeff's car parked
outside the garage and could see that he had left in their
cabin cruiser *Mageanca,* a name invented with letters out of
the children's names. She hurried back in the house so that
she could follow the boat with the binoculars.

Andy and Geoff, she could see now with the glasses,
were the figures she had seen on the beach, and she watched
as they waded out through the waves to *Mageanca* and climbed
aboard. Now it was the *Mageanca* that was no longer moving. It was stuck on the sand flats, but then a neighbor went
out in his own motorboat to help tow them off. She watched
as the men moored the boat with doubled lines. Then Jeff
brought Charlie, the neighbor, back to the house. Catherine
fixed a quick lunch for everyone. As she got up to help the
maid clear the dishes, she noticed that Jeff was slumped in
his chair at the head of the table.

"It's my heart," Jeff told his wife. "Just under my heart."

Catherine and Charlie helped Jeff struggle to the living room sofa. Catherine was thankful that Charlie was there

as she could never have gotten Jeff, a big man and also overweight, onto the sofa by herself. His pulse was so weak that she gave him a stimulant of smelling salts and called the family doctor. When the doctor arrived, he told Jeff that he would need three days of bed rest. The doctor stayed at the house for several hours to monitor Jeff's condition, until he was satisfied that his patient was stable. When he left, it was almost three o'clock.

As Catherine Moore settled her husband in bed, she watched the weather out the bedroom window. GH38 was trashing Long Island, just over the horizon, but she hadn't a clue. The sky had clouded over and there was rain tossing in the air. She dispatched her son Geoffrey and Loretta, the cook, to bring the family clothes in off the line. The wind on the water was getting wild, whipping up great shapes, beautiful and dramatic, on the ocean. Then she saw that their Herreshoff, another family sailboat, had broken loose. It appeared to be dragging anchor, moving slowly but steadily down toward the fort at the end of the bay. Without mentioning it to Jeff, she went to the children's room to check that the windows were closed tight. She did not think they should undertake another boat rescue at the moment. The rain was blowing up under the windowsills and dripping down in a stream on the east side of the house. She ran for towels and bath mats to stuff the windows and mop the floor, working frantically to keep up with the water that was coming in. Jeff was looking out the window, too. "There goes Cy's boat. I'd better call and tell him," she heard him call to her down the hall. Outside the children's window, she noticed that their slide had blown over and a chair from the beach club had landed in the yard. She was relieved to see that May Doherty, family friend and cousin, had returned home. She needed May's help.

That morning they had laid out all of Geoffrey's clothes to pack for school, but now they heaped rugs, toys, and everything else on top of them just to get it all off the wet floor. May pitched in to help with the mopping. Things were starting to feel under control when Loretta, the cook, called from downstairs. Water was coming in the dining room. She and May exchanged a look that said "What next?" before they decided to let the upstairs mopping go and take up the rugs downstairs.

Andy, who had been sent to bring home the girls, arrived at the same time with Anne, Cathy, and Margaret, bounding with energy. They had only just made it, they said breathlessly. Andy explained that it had been difficult to keep the beach wagon on the road in 30-mile-an-hour winds. He had needed to get out of the car and escort Mary Moore, the girls' cousin, to the door of her house down the road when he dropped her off because the wind was so strong he was afraid she might blow away. When he reached home with the Moore girls, the wind outside was whistling weirdly and sand was blowing into their faces. To Andy it felt like sandpaper. He groped for the garage door to lead everyone inside. The girls' cheeks were flushed with excitement. They had been soberly quiet during the precarious drive, but once inside they thrived on the sense of adventure and drama, especially the telling of it. A few telegraph poles had come down on Westerly Road, and they'd nearly been blown off the road themselves, they told Catherine, laughing, mimicking with their arms and bodies the way the car had swayed back and forth. They thought it thrilling. Anne and Cathy, the two eldest, had run down to the seawall to see the wild water before coming in the house, and they were amazed that the wind literally blew them off their feet for several seconds.

Despite the children's high spirits, the situation looked serious now to Catherine, and she suggested that everyone start out immediately for the car, but Jeff said that he and Geoffrey would stay with the house. He did not feel like traveling again, and it seemed a prime opportunity to stay behind for some time alone with his son. Geoffrey was often bursting with adolescent obstinacy these days. His father's long hours and a house full of women made occasions for father-and-son bonding hard to come by. No matter his reasoning, Catherine, nearing the end of her rope, refused to go unless everyone went. She tried to call her friend Harriet who lived down the way to get a report on the road conditions there, but the phone was dead.

While Catherine and Jeff Moore strategized over what to do next, the girls flounced around in their pinafores and hair bows, high on the storm. They squealed and chased each other around the house until their chatter wore on their mother's already frayed nerves. Catherine sent them up to the third floor. Jeff, overhearing, said it would be safer to have them ride it out in the car in the garage. It was constructed of solid concrete and would be safest, he figured, because of the strong foundation and the huge bulkhead that formed a seawall. Catherine called upstairs and told them to come down again.

At this point, the family dynamics began to rival the weather. When Anne and Margaret looked into the basement, they saw that water was starting to rise. They were horrified that their pets would be left down there and refused to go without them. So the seven cats and kittens were brought upstairs and carried out to the Buick with May and the girls. Geoffrey took Major, the Newfoundland, into the car with him. He ignored the storm and the others by burying himself in the newest Action Comic, Superman. Catherine tried to think of what they were likely to need next and ran up to the kitchen to pack bread, butter, and milk to have along in the car. She told May to play the car radio to amuse everyone and listen for any news about the weather. Then she supplied each floor of the house with bread and butter and candles and matches, in case they were to be marooned all night on any one of them.

A little before four the storm suddenly intensified. The wind was so strong that it was forcing water through the seams in the window frames, and Andy was sent upstairs to help mop up in the bedrooms. The situation seemed impossible. As fast as he and the others worked, the water came in as though from a garden hose. Water was also leaking from the attic ceiling, and the strain on the ceiling and rafters was making a weird and ghostly sound, like that of heavy furniture being scooted around overhead. In the last moment of reflection before he became frantically busy trying to deal with a series of crises, he realized he was truly scared. He headed downstairs to tell Jeff and Catherine what was happening upstairs when the waves began crashing against the second-floor windows. Jeff, though incapacitated several hours earlier, ignored the doctor's orders to not get up and began to nail the winter shutters over the broken living room window. Loretta and Catherine threw themselves against the shutters to hold them in place while he hammered. Andy ran to the basement to bring up longer nails, but even they wouldn't do the job. The wind ripped them out as soon as they pounded them in. Andy offered to go outside to try to place the shutters over the opening from the outside, but the consensus was that the wind would drive the shutters right through the window. Before they had time to attempt another approach, the wind blew the front door open. Jeff looked peaked from the exertion, so Catherine, doing her best to not overtax her husband, went down into the cellar and dragged up a door to use as a barricade. The water was up to her knees and soaked the hem of her dress. Geoff appeared to help, but his parents curtly sent him back to the safety of the garage. Then the dining room windows, three of them in one casing, broke out in one piece. The first of the big breakers to hit the house landed at full force and began to flood the basement. Catherine's heart stopped. They were in serious danger, she realized. She rushed to the garage and ordered everyone out of the car. Margaret, her youngest, she took in her arms.

She rapped on the window of the little car and told Geoffrey to get out. A storm wasn't going to deprive him of his adolescent contrariness. "Why?" he resisted, turning back to his comics. Hoping to scare him into action, she retorted, "Because the house is going to collapse." Rather than follow her, he took Major out of the car and put him in the beach wagon, parked just outside the garage. The dog

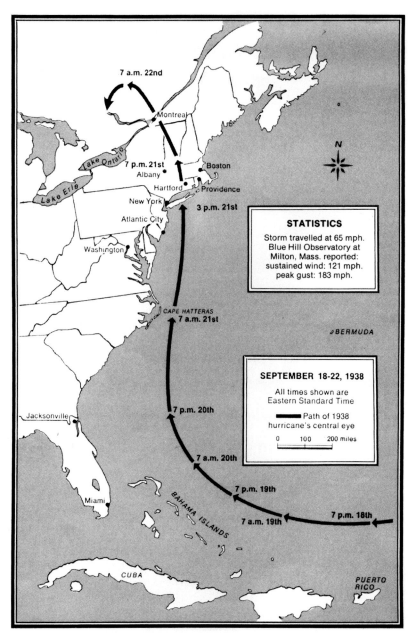

The Great Hurricane traveled unseen offshore as it made its way up the eastern seaboard, evading detection by the U.S. Weather Bureau after it passed Jacksonville, Florida. Forecasters assumed it would move out to sea, as most tropical storms did when they encountered the cooler air and water temperature in the region, but GH38 continued heading up the coast, aimed directly at Long Island. (from *Hurricane!* by Joe McCarthy [New York: American Heritage Press, 1969])

The Duryea dock on Ford Pond Bay was a model of the flourishing Long Island fishing industry in 1938. Helen Bengtson was at work in the Duryea store and office the morning before the hurricane as fishermen came through pondering ominous signs in the weather. In a matter of hours the neatly stowed boats and stacks of lobster traps would be blown to bits. (East Hampton Town Marine Museum)

Onlookers felt helpless as the wind and waves washed cars out to sea and splintered houses. In Watch Hill, Rhode Island, a car sank under a fallen telephone pole. (*Springfield Union*)

The residents of Napatree Point built their summer cottages close to the water on a point of sand that stretched out into the sea. A modest seawall was all that stood between them and the water, and Fort Road was the only way to get on and off the point. (*Tidings Magazine*)

The neat line of forty-four gray-shingled houses was swept away in a matter of hours. The following morning the point was almost a clean stretch of sand. It strained credulity, as if the cottages and lively shimmering summer life that had so recently existed had never been. (*Tidings Magazine*)

The Moore house was boasted to be one of largest and the most sturdily built cottages on Napatree Point. As the waters rose, the Geoffrey Moore family fled to the top-floor maid's room. When the roof blew off, a remnant of the floor it was attached to became the raft the group of ten set afloat on. (*Tidings Magazine*)

The sea wall, no match for the waves and surge that came with the hurricane, was all that remained along Fort Road. (from *The Search: An Account of the Fort Road Tragedy*, by Paul Johnson Moore [Westerly, R.I.: self-published, 1988])

GH38 raged up Narragansett Bay into Providence shortly after 4:00 P.M. Downtown workers heading home at the end of the day found the scene on the street unbelievable as the water rose eighteen feet in the business district. The parking lot on Pine and Eddy Streets was completely submerged minutes after the above picture was taken. Police and looters traveled by boat until the water receded at about 11:00 P.M. (from *The Great Hurricane and Tidal Wave, Rhode Island* [Providence, R.I.: Providence Journal Company, 1938])

The waterfront took a beating during the height of the storm all along the East Coast. Powerful winds drove boats onto the shore, as pictured above in Dorchester Bay in Massachusetts. Some fishing boats that had gone out to sea during the calm of morning never returned to port. (*Wide World*)

Shorefront homeowners faced the depressing task of salvage and cleanup in the days following the hurricane, as did the family amid the rubble of Misquamicut, Rhode Island, above. (*New York Daily News*)

Gone were the playgrounds of a prosperous social class emerging toward the end of the Depression. Onlookers took in the scene on the beach in Westhampton, where more than 150 houses had stood a day earlier. (*Wide World*)

would be safer outside there, he reasoned, if the house did collapse. Meanwhile, Andy was still on the first floor braced against the shutter to hold it in place when another breaker, combined with the tremendous force of the wind, knocked him flying. When he picked himself up, he could see that a raging torrent now surrounded the house, and he fled to the second floor where the rest of the household was now assembled. Catherine was gathering clothes from the closets to take with them in case they had to leave the house. She asked Andy to go down to the garage for the life preservers. When he got there, he found that the water had risen to the halfway mark, and he had to wade through it to locate three life preservers. There were ten people upstairs, waiting. Back upstairs with the family, Andy realized that Geoffrey was missing. Catherine told him that Geoffrey was still in one of the cars in the garage.

Knowing what danger Geoffrey was in, Andy went downstairs to look for him. It was now almost impossible for him to make any headway against the wind and waves on the first floor, but he finally managed to reach the basement only to find the door into the garage jammed shut. The coal shovel that Catherine had used to hold the door open had been knocked away and the pressure of the water inside prevented entry. The only way to get into the garage now was to smash in a panel of the door. Desperate to get to Geoffrey before another breaker hit, he stepped back six or seven steps and charged the door. It bounced him back half the distance and deeply bruised his shoulder, but the door gave enough that he could now break a hole in it large enough to squeeze through. There were two cars in the garage, but only the cat and six kittens were inside. The outside garage doors had washed away at this point, and Andy looked out at the beach wagon, where he could see Geoffrey sitting the backseat. He struggled out to the car and could see that Major, the Newfoundland, was frightened out of his wits by the howling wind and rain. Geoffrey refused to leave the dog, so Andy reasoned with him to bring his pet, but Major wouldn't budge. When Geoffrey tried to pull him along, the dog bit him. Andy finally convinced him that the situation was so severe that he should leave the dog, but just as he stepped out of the car, a huge wave broke over the young men and carried them nearly to the bay. They fought their way back to the house in waist-high water, struggling to make it before the next wave hit.

Meanwhile, Jeff had his back to the front door. It had blown in despite being locked, and he was trying with all his strength to hold back the water. It was a moment that impressed ten-year-old Anne. She realized it was not just the storm that her father was trying to keep out, but that he was trying to push back the whole ocean. She thought that they were probably going to die.

The ocean pushed past Jeff into the living room, and the children fled to the next flight up, where Catherine told them to stay. It seemed safest there because it was on the side of the house away from the force of the storm, and it was the only room not leaking. She rushed back downstairs to help Jeff push the dining room table and chairs up against the front door. Nothing, however, would stanch the tons of water being hurled against the house. They gave up and ran upstairs.

Andy and Geoff managed to squeeze back into the house through the hole in the garage door and grapple their way along the hall, up the stairs, and over the chairs and tables in the front hall. Water was pouring through the breached door and cascaded over the furniture like a waterfall.

From upstairs where they were gathered, the family watched the Butler house next door blow over. The adults said nothing, but the children had seen it, too, and they began to cry that they did not want to die. Catherine calmly told them that they would not die, but that they might have to swim. Margaret and Cathy kept crying, and Margaret howled that she didn't want to swim. Their mother tried to take their minds off what they had just seen by offering them milk and bread to eat. The girls refused, but their mother and May took drinks, and then May knelt down and started to recite the Rosary. At the same time Jim Nestor, Mrs. Butler's eighteen-year-old-nephew, arrived at the house gasping for breath and clad only in his underwear. He had slipped through the smashed garage door behind Andy and Geoff. "Where are the others?" Jeff asked, referring to Jim's aunt and the maid who had been with her in the house. Jim answered, "They are gone." The children gaped. "Gone?" Andy, too, had seen the Butler house topple and go, but he had been so focused on his own struggle to get back to the house with Geoffrey that the tragedy had not yet sunk in. A short while earlier they had all looked over and seen the Butlers anxiously watching the storm from their porch. The horror of the event gripped Catherine, and she decided that she and her family would probably die, too, but she said nothing. There was nothing to say.

"What shall we do?" asked Jim.

Jeff told everyone to stay together no matter what happened. They decided it would be best to stand between the upstairs family room and the hall, hoping that the door frame would protect them if the house crashed down on them. May prayed aloud in a firm and confident voice as she clutched a picture of Christ. Cathy went to her mother. "Mummy, if I must die, I want my rosary," she said. Catherine took her into the master bedroom across the hall and found a little blue rosary. She told her to put it over her head, but it wouldn't fit, so her mother wound it around her wrist.

There were no more outcries from Cathy. She was quiet and just waited. Margaret, too, said nothing now, but kept her hand in her mother's. They all stood soberly, wondering what would come next. Loretta asked Catherine if she didn't want her pocketbook, but Catherine told her it didn't matter, that material things just didn't count anymore. Then she told everybody to take off their shoes, in case they were going to have to swim. The sight of the girls' shoes set neatly in a row made Catherine want to weep. She drew her sweater tightly around her and shoved her hands into the pockets.

She assigned everyone a buddy to look after, taking Margaret herself. She also put coats and the three life preservers on Margaret and Cathy and her cousin May. She asked Geoffrey, who was barechested at this point, to put on a sweater, but he managed to not obey. Then she told everyone, particularly the girls, to grab some large floating object if they found themselves in the water. There was no panic, but a sense of resigned calm. They prayed constantly, sometimes silently and sometimes aloud, waiting.

The group watched a tremendous wave crash against the house. The pathos and uncertainty in waiting made Andy Pupolo think he would jump out of his skin. He crept down to the foot of the stairs to see what the situation looked like below. The huge seawall was gone and the basement and front of the house had vanished. He stood paralyzed by the spectacle of the swirling, angry water. It seemed alive to him and as if it were looking for prey. Catherine peered down and watched some nice new pink curtains wash out of the linen closet, but the main thing she saw was a raging ocean where the girls' room had been at the foot of the stairs. Then another wave hit close by and covered Andy with spray. He was jarred from his stupor by the sight of a gigantic wave bearing down on the house. Its huge shadow darkened everything around it as it approached. Andy turned and ran upstairs for his life. He yelled that everyone should get to the attic.

Suddenly the house began to collapse beneath them. Quickly they ran together as a unit, down the hall and up the stairs to the third floor, and just in time, for the second floor had crumbled, slipping a little sideways as it went. They experienced the otherworldly sensation of the house in a fifteen-foot free fall as it went straight down when the water yanked the supports and foundation out from beneath it. Everyone was thrown to the floor when it landed. On the shuddering third floor, they gripped the stair railing for support. Andy warned them to keep away from the stairway, that it would go next.

With a V-shaped roof over their heads, windows at each end that might break in at any moment and trap them in the middle, and danger that the floor beneath them might

give way, they looked for an escape. Anne suggested they
tie a rope around her waist so she could swim for help. It
was a typically brave little gesture from Anne, thought her
mother. As the adults debated whether or not to break the
bathroom window and climb out, the children prepared to
face death. Anne had begun to think about heaven. She had
been taught to believe it was where she was going, and she
did believe. She led Margaret through the Act of Contrition,
asking her younger sister to repeat after her. "Oh my God,
I am heartily sorry." "I am heartily sorry." "For having offended Thee." "For having offended Thee." The adults listened to the singsong voices above the yowl of the wind and
plotted their next move. The girls wanted to swim.

Loretta, the cook, stood between Andy and the window, blocking his every move. Finally she grabbed onto his
arm and wouldn't let go. In a confessional tone, she told him
that she couldn't swim and begged him not to leave her. He
tried to convince her that she would be safest with the rest
of the group, that she could not stay behind if they had to
go into the water. Catherine asked what could be done. Andy
extricated himself from Loretta's grip and went down the attic
stairs to appraise the situation. The house seemed to be standing on nothing. The water danced beneath them and the
waves were rolling toward them with no sign of abating. The
long shadow of a towering wave that seemed even larger than
the last giant was steadily approaching. Andy called to Jeff
to come see the spectacle for himself. Jeff saw it, too, and
returned to the attic. Andy realized without question that he
was going to die and began to wonder if it would be quick or
if he would have to fight the water for his salvation. When

he made it back to the attic, Jeff Moore was saying his last farewell to his family. Jeff bent down to nuzzle his wife's cheek and looked at her directly. "Good-bye," he whispered. Catherine, teary but staunchly determined to survive, shook her head and told him not to give up yet.

They decided to make a break for it, and Jeff smashed the bathroom window. A torrent of water poured through the hole. "Should I go first?" Anne asked. Before her father could answer, the roof over their heads blew off with a piece of the floor attached to it. As if by reflex the family made for it, finding the section of floor to be a perfect raft, with two iron pipes sticking through it. Catherine caught hold of one piece and, holding Cathy tightly by the hand, climbed on. Jeff had taken Margaret in his arms and sat astride one pipe. Cathy held onto his other knee. May sat between Jeff and Catherine, holding his arm, and Anne held onto him from the back. Loretta, Jim, and Nancy managed to cling to the group and the floor, and Geoffrey and Andy sat out in front. Loretta, out of sheer terror, seemed to have given up, so Jeff told Nancy, the hired girl from the kitchen, to hold tight to her. Their house had been the last house to go, so there was nothing around them but wreckage, and the size of the waves crashing over them suggested that they were heading into the ocean. On their raft with a piece of the attic roof still attached like a sail, they made a sort of Robinson Crusoe tableau. Geoffrey said he saw sharks following.

The angled fragment of roof also caught the air like a sail, and in each gust of wind the raft was lifted into the air. During the lull between blasts it would crash back down onto the water. The only bit of absurdity came from the family parrot, which had taken refuge in the peak of the roof when the cook let her go. "Hello Polly," called the terrified parrot. Andy and Jimmy tried to detach the roof in fear that it would flip the raft or, worse, drive them out to sea. They needn't have bothered because a mighty gust of wind ripped it off completely a moment later. They were too disoriented to know what direction they were headed in and assumed they were being blown out to sea. Constantly drenched by spray, torn by the wind, and bounced about by wild waves, the fortunate eleven were driven, unknowingly, across the bay. Yet the high, angry waves that broke overhead furthered the notion that they were being blown into the Atlantic Ocean. They recited their Rosaries, dug fingernails into the shingles of the roof, and prepared to meet their God.[11]

XI

By four the weather was worsening with alarming speed all along the mainland coast, though in every town and community the residents thought their disturbances were mostly local. Polly Cleaveland and Fanny Hebert stopped for tea before starting back to Groton Long Point from Noank, but it was too wet and windy for their customary walk on the boardwalk. Bonnie Lassie stayed in the car.

The women assumed that the storm wouldn't last much longer and it would be safe to return to the cottage even though it had begun raining harder. The wind lashed the tree branches and the rain danced on the Pawcatuck River that ran along the low and narrow part of the road they traveled back to the house. The surge, rising twenty-one feet out of the ocean and funneled to a depth of fifty feet in some waterways, rose up the river like a wall of gray and brown water and took them completely by surprise. It picked up their car like a child's tub toy before tossing it into a bog two hundred feet off the road, where it rested.

Jean Cleaveland was working in her father's dentist
office when the storm hit Springfield. She'd had time to
read the local newspaper ads at her desk during lunch.
Pedestal shoes were proclaimed the new international sensation. Spencer's, the shoe store down the street, had them
on sale for $2.75. She considered slipping out for a look, but
it was raining hard. The last appointment of the day had
called to cancel, saying the weather was too ominous. Jean
stepped outside to see. The sky was dark, all right. The water
in the curbs downtown was getting deep. She and her father closed the office just before five and started the walk
home together. It was the first time they were sorry that
Polly had taken the car. The wind was so strong by the time
they came to the flat, parklike area on the way home that
they were struggling to stay upright. Jean, who weighed
barely a hundred pounds, was having a particularly difficult time keeping to the sidewalk. "Get down!" shouted
Harold when the wind reached a new peak. Then he lay on
top of her as the wind blew its worst. They laughed about it
a little, but Jean was scared. When the wind subsided and
the air was full of the smell that follows behind rain on dry
soil and grass, they ran for home. The power and lights were
both out when they got there. Safely inside, they finally
spoke of what was on both of their minds: her mother. Their
phones still worked, but the operator explained that all lines
were out along the coastline.

As GH38 wound off Long Island Sound and struck the
mainland, its force extended inland into New England so
that residents as far north as Pascoag, Rhode Island, forty
miles from the ocean, were terrified by the wind and sound,

like a freight train's scream, that drove schoolchildren to bury their heads under blankets and sofa pillows to escape its horrifying sound. Residents in Manchester, New Hampshire, 130 miles inland to the north, watched their windows ripple in and out like waves in the wind and pressure. Power outages shut down the mills along the Merrimack River and workers were stranded without bridges and streetcars. As the leafy oaks and maples fell, silently it seemed because the air itself was howling so loudly, only the chestnut trees, whose leaves had fallen or were blown off, were spared and remained standing like skeletons.

The eastern Connecticut coastline had taken a pummeling, but the hurricane's attack was still building. It dealt the picture-perfect Connecticut coastal village of Stonington a particularly serious blow. There was hardly time for caution before the storm struck the waterfront there. Workers were sent home in the nick of time when a smokestack above the Atwood Machine Company (ATCO), a big brick building on the edge of the harbor, began weaving in the wind. All the windows blew out and tons of sand were blown into the building. Workers on their way out watched in amazement as the sidewalk in front of the building was lifted by the wind and water, and many had to straddle and scramble across fallen trees to pick their way home to higher ground.

As the water began to rise on nearby Wall Street, a main thoroughfare on the waterfront, its residents fled. The Starr family, who lived on Wall, left with their neighbors in the belief that they would return after several feet of flooding subsided. But when it began to look as if their homes might be washed away, two Starr family members went back to get their money out of the house. They didn't trust banks and kept their savings at home.

Anna Sisk, twenty-one, was working in her father's grocery store on Hancock Street in downtown Stonington when the storm began to hit hard. She had been clerking alongside her father when a man came in to tell him that the force of the wind had broken a window in their house, around the corner from the store. Her father took off to make repairs and left Anna in charge. She had Bijou, her gorgeous white chow dog, to keep her company. The door to the back room had blown shut in the wind, shutting Bijou in it. The dog barked, and when she opened the door to let him back into the store, she saw the whole back room pulling away from the front, carried by a wave that had risen underneath the store. Nothing but waves were back there now, and Anna froze for a second, the sight was so unbelievable. Absolutely beautiful but scary, she thought. The back of the building was gone and she could look right onto the water. And then she saw and felt what was coming. The wind was tremendous, and a huge wave, like a blue-gray wall with white atop that looked as high as the building, was coming right at her. In a heartbeat she decided to forget the store, grabbed the dog, and fled out the front door. Just as she turned the corner to head up the hill to her house on Main Street, the big wave hit. It would overtake her, she saw, so she plunged into water up to her chin and held tight to the dog's collar. She and her dog, swimming strongly together, made it from the street to the steps to their house, and miraculously, as it turned out, this was the high-water mark of the hurricane in Stonington. The storm tide had been over fourteen feet. She paused to

look back and saw that the store had been picked up by the
wave and hurled into the middle of the main street, where
it landed and acted as a barrier against the wind and high
water in that area. But the wind was still tremendous, and
she thought as she hurried on that if the store had not ended
up in that spot, she and Bijou would most probably have
been washed out to sea.

When Anna and her dog reached home, citizens were
going from door to door telling all the residents to get to
higher ground. The Baptist church on Main Street was open
and everyone seemed headed there. Her father chose to stay
behind to keep making repairs to the house and to stay with
her grandfather, whose failing eyesight made it preferable
for him to stay in the house. They were also worried about
her older brother, a bass fiddler in a dance band, who had
gone up to Ocean Beach in New London that day for a re-
hearsal. Her father would stay and wait in case Ed came
home, but he instructed Anna to gather up her sister Caroline,
nine, and her dog Bijou, and go to the church.

Caroline needed comforting. She was soaking wet and
crying from fear, and she depended on Anna, who had taken
care of her since their mother's death five years before. Anna
helped her pick her way carefully across all the fallen electrical wires. Anna was amazed and disheartened by all the
downed wires and trees. Stonington, such a picturesque
little New England town, looked demolished. The only thing
that took her mind off the calamity was being inside the
Baptist church. She was Catholic and had never been inside the big protestant sanctuary before. The novelty and
sense of being inside a heretofore forbidden place was a

distraction and relief. She and Caroline settled into the pews, where soft drinks and cookies, sent over by a neighboring store, were passed around. There were stories about all the windows in the borough school blowing out. The teachers had marched the students from twelve grades up the hill to the library, which sat in the town square at the highest point in town. The hurricane seemed a cruel and abrupt end to a social season that had been enormous fun for most of Anna's age group. Every Sunday they dressed up and went to Ocean Beach to hear Artie Shaw and sometimes even Billie Holiday. Anna wondered about her friend John Donahy, who worked as an apprentice at ATCO. She had taught John to dance and was learning to sing the blues herself. John flattered her by saying she sounded like Ella Fitzgerald.

John Donahy had made it out of ATCO safely and was with friends in Ernie's Tavern, drinking by gaslight, relieved to find that the tap in the beer keg was working when everything else, including the lights and phones, wasn't. Word began trickling in that the entire Stonington fishing fleet, some fifty-plus boats, had been destroyed in the harbor. They also heard that the Starrs, who had gone back to their house to get their savings from their house on the waterfront, had drowned when the surge hit Wall Street.

XII

Tiny Rhode Island, forty miles wide and fifty miles long with its center hollowed out by Narragansett Bay and a collage of small islands, sat directly in the hurricane's path. Napatree, barely more than a sandspit delicately framing Little Narragansett Bay, was host to forty-two cottages, most of them built in a prim line facing out to sea only a few feet back from the seawall. Thirty-nine people were in residence on Wednesday afternoon. None of them had the slightest idea as they went about their revelries and end-of-season chores that they were poised directly in the coming hurricane's path. Most of them went about life as usual until well after lunchtime. One woman hostessed a luncheon on the rocks until the wind broke it up at 2:30, at which time some of her departing guests discovered that they were trapped by fallen trees blocking the road back to the mainland. Yet most of them easily believed the storm would pass, that they would be merely inconvenienced, that they should even make the most of an opportunity to prolong the festive mood and party. None imagined that by five o'clock, desperate events would be occurring up and down the bay as the hurricane hit with peak intensity.

Excitement gave way to terror for Mae Lowry and the members of the Christ Episcopal Church Mother's Club. They had been in high spirits when the servants for the Wells family loaded up the family car and drove away. The group of women had gaily moved into the Wells' house on the ocean side of the road to gain the protection of the more substantial house and for the dramatic view it offered of the ocean during the storm. They were enjoying a small sense of daring. They saw the waves, ever higher, blow over the dunes toward them.

It is assumed, because they chose to stay, that they initially thought the wind and rising surf were merely a thrilling spectacle, but the moment surely came when they realized first their danger and then, with no escape possible, the inevitability of their deaths. Whether they took comfort calmly in the tenets of the faith that the Reverend Tobin had extolled during their special church service a few hours before or whether the water caught them suddenly, we do not know. They may have even become transfixed and terrified by the elements overtaking them. These were the thoughts that would haunt Mae's husband, David Lowry, a plumber in Westerly.

It had been about three o'clock when Lowry walked over to the Christ Church rectory in Westerly, located around the corner from his home. He found Reverend Tobin's son Jack there, home from college.

Jack had just returned from a frightening trip around town. He had taken a girlfriend and gone into Watch Hill earlier in the day and seen the wind howl down Bay Street in front of the shops, the yacht club, and the dock. They could see clear across to the entrance to Stonington's harbor from there. Jack had parked his Ford coupe on the bay side of the street, but when they watched the roof of the Plimpton Hotel blow away over their heads in one piece, they began to question if they should be out in such weather. After a slate shingle whistled through the air and buried itself in the side of Jack's car, they decided it was time to get out of there. Jack and his date managed to get back on the road to Westerly, but others on the waterfront soon discovered they had few options. A surge of ocean water stranded people on the Watch Hill beachway. The captain of a nineteen-foot cabin boat tried to help them across to shore with a rope, but only three or four managed to make it. Bystanders onshore watched the water rise fast along the storefronts on the main street, and a few ran into Sisson's, a waterfront restaurant. The water kept rising until the owners and remaining customers rushed up to the second floor, where they could look out the front windows onto the harbor. They watched the yacht club wash out to sea and the neighboring beach cottages blow away like boxes made of matchsticks. But again it was the screeching sound of the tin roof blowing off the marquis front of the Plimpton Hotel, hearing the sound of nails popping and shearing, and seeing the massive metal sheet hurl into the air with a shrill wail that most terrified the watchers. Several women became hysterical, screaming and tearing at their hair until two teenage boys with a Model A offered them a ride if they could make it to the car. They began the drive uphill to Ocean View Avenue, along which the largest homes perched like aeries looking out to sea. A gust of wind tore at the top of the car in another cacophony of flying debris and metal. That was the last straw. The women jumped out and ran away. The boys never saw them again.

After leaving Watch Hill, Jack Tobin had dropped his date home and returned to Elm Street, the big beautiful tree-lined street of Victorian and Greek Revival houses at the top of downtown Westerly, where the trees, still in full leaf, were deeply bent by the wind. He was relieved to arrive home safely. Initially, he was reluctant to head out again with David Lowry, but the man was a member of his father's parish, and David's anguish was so apparent that Jack agreed to go out with him to search for his wife even though the storm was still raging. When they reached the golf course across from the pond behind the Lowry house in David's pickup truck, they could see that the ocean water had come that far inland. They spotted what they thought was debris lying on the fairway, but as they drew closer, they could see that most of the forms were bodies. David, nearly crazed by now, stopped the truck and jumped out of the cab. He thought the first woman's body he saw was Mae's, and he ran to give her artificial resuscitation before he realized that the tangled, swollen corpse wasn't her. They blundered along that way until they had discovered six of the seven women's bodies. Mae's was among those that the two men loaded into the truck and drove to the high school, now serving as a morgue, across from the church. Young Tobin, a medical student at Yale at the time, would go on to serve as a medic during the war on America's horizon. During his three years as a military medic he would see many dead bodies and gruesome casualties, but they would never have the visceral impact and stunning sense of tragedy that he experienced on the golf course helping Mae Lowry's grief-stricken husband gather her and the other hurricane victims into the truck.

*　*　*

It was feisty Helen Joy Lee who swam daily with a thermometer in her mouth off of Napatree Point, to the amusement of Catherine Moore and her girls, who knew exactly what time the hurricane hit the coast. She boasted the newest of inventions: a waterproof wristwatch. She had taken her usual morning swim that day at eleven and then gone home to wash the dog, a splendid German shepherd. Her daughter and two friends took the car and left for the day. At three, Helen thought it was still nice enough to walk to the village, but she found she was mistaken once she set out. The blowing sand stung her legs and she turned back. She watched sailboats struggling against the high wind in the bay and saw the Moore family's Herreshoff sailboat being blown along, dragging its anchor toward the fort at the end of the road. At 3:30 the wind veered to the south and for ten minutes there were no whitecaps, though Helen thought the sea looked like green cake batter having white milk stirred into it with a spoon. Then the wind came up and the surf began to pound. Salt spray and sand were being driven under her front door. An upstairs window was blown in, and water poured down onto the ground floor landing from another unidentifiable leak. For the next half hour there was nothing to do but wait to see what the weather was going to do. The water and wind driving against the windows on the east side made it impossible to see anything in that direction. On the west side she watched the chimney of the house next door fall onto the roof and the front porch and porch posts below disappear into the wind. Fifteen minutes of stillness followed.

Helen assumed the storm center was passing and that a violent wind would follow, but she also believed the wind would then decrease. Donning her raincoat, she went out onto the back porch just as the glass in the front door broke and the back door slammed shut behind her. Her first thought was her pets. The dog was tied to the inside of the back door, and she slipped the kitten into her coat pocket to protect him from the wind, but a strong gust twisted her lightweight coat with such force that the kitten was tossed up into the air. Unable to open the back door against the wind and water, she pulled the dog through its broken window. With a log from the woodpile, she battered a crack in the door so that the water, now a foot deep, could run out.

Her watch read 4:30. She sat on the woodpile with the dog and wondered how much longer the wind would go on, and then the water attacked her. There was a loud crashing sound from the front of the house and a wave washed right into her lap. A piece of debris from the porch broke her left arm as the swell lifted her and the dog into the bay. It was all she could do to dodge the debris, first the lattice off her own porch and then pieces of sidewalk. She managed to unleash the dog, which disappeared, but the kitten was floating on a board nearby. It was beginning to look like she was going to have to swim, so Helen struggled out of her raincoat with her injured arm. She was wearing shorts and a sweater underneath.

The heavy debris in the water was a serious threat to even as strong a swimmer as Helen. Two floating barn doors threatened to crush her chest. At one point she climbed onto a porch roof despite her bad arm, but it eventually capsized, so she seized a smaller piece to hang onto. A large chunk of wood hit her in the head repeatedly and blackened her eye. Lying in the trough of a wave, she could see shutters, chairs, and pillows being blown off the wave tops. When the rooftop that had capsized returned with the point up, she crawled onto it for protection. Then a mattress floated by, and she moved onto it. The wind seemed to decrease slightly. A broken boat looked like an even better thing to ride on, so she climbed on and was amazed when she realized it was carrying her over the tops of trees. A few of their boughs were visible sticking out of the water. Ten minutes later the boat washed ashore in growing darkness. The water reached Helen's armpits. She found a tree limb at water level that she could hang onto. Her watch said it was 6:30 and she stayed there, hanging on until the water receded as low as her feet so she could begin to climb down. By then it was 8:00 P.M. She believed she had reached Connecticut, but she had been blown onto Barn Island, just off the Rhode Island shoreline.[12]

❊ ❊ ❊

The Moore family, afloat in the bay, continued to believe they were washing out to sea. Their situation seemed desperate until Jeff Moore caught a glimpse of telephone poles sticking out of the water. He recognized their location, and a wave of hopefulness flooded over him. The poles stood at the edge of Little Narragansett Bay. While the family had not truly reached safety yet, he felt enough relief to attempt a moment of lightheartedness, mostly for the children's sake. "Do you have your false teeth on?" he asked May. "I lost them," she answered, a bit chagrined. "I know, I've been sitting on them all the way," he joked. The girls broke into laughter. Perhaps Catherine appreciated best how amazing his exertions and fortitude were following a heart episode that morning.

Then they spotted what they thought was land in the hazy distance, but as they began to rejoice, the floor of their raft buckled. Catherine silently concluded that this was the end after all, that they didn't have a chance of surviving in water as wild and debris-laden as the surge swirling around them. Then their raft struck ground. It split in two as they scrambled off, reminding them to the very last minute of how narrow their escape had been. The feeling of relief that swept over them was almost incapacitating. They were totally exhausted, and stunned by their good fortune.

They, like Helen Joy, had blown north onto Barn Island, where a haystack, or rather a collapsed barn that once sheltered hay, provided some protection from wind that was still bending the trees to the ground. At first they looked for an escape from the island, but the channel that was usually a few feet wide on the north side of Barn Island had become a torrent several hundred feet wide.

It was dark, and though they were relieved to be off the water, they did not yet feel their survival was certain. Exposure and cold were the next hazards, so they covered each other with hay to stay warm during the night. Eventually the stars came out and the wind died enough so they could listen for the sound of any passing motors. They did not know that the catastrophe was so far-reaching that the whole shoreline had been disabled. They saw a glow on the horizon that looked like a fire and they assumed, wrongly, that it was in Stonington, several miles away. There would be no rescue that night.

* * *

All afternoon the storm intensified in the town of Narragansett, at the western edge of the opening of Narragansett Bay where it meets Rhode Island Sound and faces out to the Atlantic Ocean. On the southwestern horizon offshore, obscured by spray and clouds, lay Block Island and, just beyond it, Montauk and eastern Long Island, which were being pummeled into a coma by the storm. To the right, along the coast, Connecticut was being battered. The Rhode Islanders, innocent of the devastation, simply remarked that they were having "quite a blow." They had no idea that the wind, as it cleared Long Island, was driving a fifty-foot surge that would flood their shoreline, just as it was engulfing the Connecticut coast, and swallow some of them whole.

Nearly everyone but the dozen employees had left the Dunes Club where Aclon Coggeshall worked. One member, a man who wintered in Florida, had stood surveying the waterfront and sky after lunch. In addition to the wind and rain, he noted a green tint to the sky. "This is a hurricane," Aclon heard him say. He and the other club employees were too busy scurrying around trying to clear the waterfront and tie everything down to think much about what a hurricane was or wasn't. To the best of Aclon's knowledge, it was a big storm, something like a nor'easter. He wondered if the man from Florida wasn't overstating matters a bit. Aclon didn't think hurricanes came to New England.

He and the bathhouse manager had moved the outdoor furniture in and closed the cabanas. Club member John Norris and his elderly mother were the last clients to leave. They had seemed not to want to go, hoping after lunch that the storm would pass, but now they were going, even though several of the staff suggested that perhaps they should wait now until the weather — and driving conditions — improved. However, Mrs. Norris wanted to go, and if employees of the Dunes were used to anything, it was that you didn't argue with club members, especially older women. They watched them go. With the club closed and secured, the employees decided it was time to leave. Water was waist-high in the parking lot, so they decided to swim across it to get inland to higher ground. It was a lark until the 110-by-40-foot metal roof from the clubhouse ripped free with a screeching yowl and landed in the water several feel in front of them. They could feel the concussion as it hit the water. Aclon knew that they were spared only by the grace of God. He was sure he would have been beheaded if the roof had landed a few feet closer. For the first time, fear settled in the pit of his stomach. Everyone in the group seemed to feel it, too, and they swam now toward higher ground with a new sense of urgency. Aclon wondered about his family. His father was working in Providence that day and his mother had gone to visit relatives in Massachusetts. He thought things must be bad down by the twin towers, the landmark structures on the seawall downtown in Narragansett, near where his buddy Bill Northup typically hung out when he wasn't busy driving a grocery truck.

The hurricane's surge was a juggernaut by the time it hit Narragansett Bay, taking beaches, homes, lighthouses, boats, bathing pavilions, and in some cases lives with it. Aclon's buddy Bill was in the Surf Garage behind the Surf Hotel on Narragansett Avenue when the hurricane hit. He and his friends typically hung out there with their friend, Red Merney, who ran the garage. About 3:30, Red looked up from under the hood of a car he'd just finished servicing. The wind was blowing hard, so he and the others decided to close up the shop and go over and have a look at the water. The waterfront was two blocks away. As they walked by the Surf Hotel pool, they saw that the ocean had risen over the boardwalk between it and the ocean, and waves were breaking into the pool. Red was worried that the water would reach the garage. The young men realized that the granite block seawall at Narragansett Pier had given way to the wind and water, and they had their first inkling of the hurricane's raw force and power. Awed, they decided to turn back.

Just as they reached the garage, Bill's father arrived in his blue 1928 Buick. Red told him to put the car on the lift to keep it high and dry. The water was rising fast in the garage, but just as he turned on the jack to raise it, the power went out. Tom Scan grabbed the accounting books and cash register and put them on the windowsill in the bathroom to keep them dry. In the commotion, Red forgot that the three fifty-gallon drums with pumps were only half filled with oil. They emptied themselves into the now nearly hip-high water, covering the men in a black, oily slick. Bill's father, a short man, was up to his neck in water when they decided to leave for higher ground. Bill and his friend helped guide him and his chihuahua dog, tucked under his arm, along the climb up Narragansett Avenue. They were a sight, all soaking wet and oily.

It was a two-mile walk to Red's place in Peacedale, where they could shower and put on dry clothes. Safe and dry, the young men climbed into Red's truck and went back downtown to see if they could help. They suspected that Mrs. Woolley, whom they called Ma, the owner of the Surf Hotel, was stranded. They found a rowboat and rowed over to the hotel, where the water was so deep that they could row right alongside a second-story window. "Mrs. Woolley, are you all right? We've come to get you," they called through the window. Ma came over to talk to them. "I'm staying right where I am," she said defiantly but with a smile. Then she asked them to bring her some cigarettes. The men explained that all the stores were flooded, and rowed over to a boardinghouse where Mr. Kaplan, a popular resident, was marooned on the roof. He said he was planning to stay up there, that he'd just climbed up to see the water and keep dry. They looked at each other, baffled that their rescue attempts were being rebuffed, and rowed away up the avenue.

* * *

Jamestown, twelve miles across the opening of Narragansett Bay from Newport, was more than miles away from the opulence and grandeur of the fortunes that had built Newport. In Newport the mansions, though called "cottages," had been built mostly with railroad and industrial fortunes. They sheltered the wealthy and socially prominent from Philadelphia

and New York every summer. Jamestown was a flourishing summer colony as well, but come September it reverted
to a typical, somewhat depressed, year-round Rhode Island
shoreline town where most of its residents either farmed,
fished, or worked at menial jobs. Since the turn of the century, a sizable number had been Portuguese, mostly emi-
grants from the Azores.

On Conimicut Point farther up Narragansett Bay, the
many islands, peninsulas, and points were visible from one
shoreline to the other. In Shawomet the residents liked to
walk along the point, especially at night when they could
see the lights of the bridge between Barrington and Bristol
twinkle nearby in the dark.

※ ※ ※

Off Conanicut Island, which lies in the middle of the bay,
was the Plum Beach lighthouse, facing sternly down the
channel. It was built on a sandy shoal in 1897 to warn ships
off the rocks and narrow passageway down the western lobe
of Narragansett Bay. Though the towns and villages that
dotted the numerous coastlines of so many peninsulas and
points were protected by lying within the seemingly sheltered mouth of the Atlantic Ocean where it met Rhode
Island Sound, the waters surrounding them could be treacherous and had claimed lives and cargo before the lighthouse
was erected. It was a triumph of nineteenth-century engineering, with a cast-iron caisson sunk more than ninety feet
into the floor of Narragansett Bay to anchor the lighthouse.
Now it was put to the test.

Edwin Babcock was the substitute lighthouse keeper

for the Plum Beach light, and on the afternoon of September 21 he planned to return to his restaurant-grocery-tourist cabin business on the mainland where his wife and daughter were waiting for him. At 2:30 he tried to row his dory to shore, but the stiff breeze made rowing impossible. He was getting nowhere, so he tied the boat to the dock and returned to the lighthouse. His helper, Johnny Ganze, twenty-nine, was watching from the steps. Ganze had been stationed at the Sakonnet Point light previously, and he'd hated it. Fierce storms were more common that far out to sea, and he always felt harassed by the wind and rising waves. He was happy to be reassigned to Plum Beach.

When Babcock climbed up to where Ganze was standing, the two of them looked down the bay at the ferry *Hammonton,* a mile or so away. It was headed across the West Passage from Jamestown to Saunderstown, and the quartermaster was trying to guide it around the north end of Dutch Island toward Saunderstown. Before he got as far as the red bell buoy north of Dutch Island, he gave up and headed back to the slip at Jamestown.

Within a matter of minutes the visibility from the lighthouse diminished markedly, and they watched as the ferry slipped out of their sight. The waves were pounding ten feet above the riprap onto the galley deck when they barricaded themselves into the kitchen on the same level, but the unabated wind and waves kept the men from feeling safe. Within the half hour they grabbed a portable radio, flashlight, and a flask of whiskey and headed up the spiral staircase to the keeper's quarters.

By now the fury of the storm was striking the point. The waves smashed higher against the lighthouse than either man had ever seen before. Babcock, more of a talker, told Ganze that he was scared. Ganze, more stoic, insisted that he had seen worse storms at Sakonnet Point.

As conditions seemed to be going from bad to worse, Babcock looked out the east window and watched a sailing yacht stream by at an unimaginably fast clip. It was the *Moby Dick*, a forty-foot sloop from the Saunderstown Yacht Club. He pointed the boat out to Ganze, who leaned over and gave him a pull on the whiskey bottle.

The water had risen fifteen feet above the usual high tide mark, and Ganze and Babcock climbed higher up into the lighthouse. Somehow, it felt safer. They went to the fourth level, Ganze's living quarters, from where they could see shacks, boats, and houses zooming by in the wind on the water. It was unbelievable. Babcock felt sick. Ganze was still able to get high on the excitement. In a show of fearlessness, he stepped onto the edge of the foundation that encircled the lighthouse at the main deck galley.

He watched as thirty-foot waves broke open the kitchen door and the portholes to the basement below. He and Babcock watched the icebox swirl away into the bay. Even the coal stove was picked up and moved. It was more alarming to watch their boats, the once only plausible means of escape, be blown up the bay. Unspeaking, they climbed up to the fog-bell room, on the fifth level. There was no place else to go. They were now forty-five feet above the riprap. The lighthouse began to vibrate and rattle from the pressure of the wind and water. Suddenly even Ganze was afraid.

He fixed his concern on the main light, a heavy lens apparatus and rotating device. If it fell, the damage would be devastating. The base of the lantern was filled with kerosene covered with a thick film of mercury upon which the lantern, when lit, revolved. He worried that the vibration from the storm could jolt the lantern.

In desperation, Ganze pulled shut the iron trap door that separated them from the chamber where the lantern sat above. He bolted it shut and then took a coil of rope and threw it at Babcock. They worked together to lash themselves back-to-back against the pipe that contained the clockwork weights that ran from the lantern's chamber down to the basement. If the lighthouse toppled, as they feared it would, they would at least be together—dead or alive.[13]

❖ ❖ ❖

Ashore, Jamestown was suffering a tragedy that the town would never get over. The community's one school bus, loaded with eight elementary school children, stalled in the floodwaters midway across the causeway of Mackerel Cove. Norm Caswell, the driver, took the children off the bus and instructed them to form a line holding hands, but a wall of water marching in from the bay reached the stranded vehicle. It lifted some of the children onto the roof of the bus, and as their parents looked on and watched them scramble in terror, the water swept on and closed over them. Only the bus driver and one child survived.[14]

In contrast to the stark Jamestown tragedy, another quite different rescue took place across the channel in Newport. Pierrepoint Johnson Jr., three-year-old son of Mr. and Mrs. Pierrepoint Johnson of New York and Newport, was in danger. The family nurse, cook, and gardener were with the toddler in a seaside "cottage," a typical Newport mansion, when the storm struck, knocking out the phone and washing away the automobile they might have escaped in. Fortunately, the gardener had phoned for help seconds before the wave came that knocked out all communications, and the lieutenant commander of the naval training station who received his call intervened. A rescue plea to the Coast Guard was not an option, but he was able to reach officers at the Fort Adams army post at the mouth of the harbor. When the rescuers arrived, they saw that the gardener had tied bedsheets together and was lowering the child and his nurse to a nearby rock outcropping because the foundation of the house was beginning to collapse under the force of the waves. The rescue party had to run lifelines to three houses in order to secure its position. Then the officers waded and swam, risking their lives to reach the stranded group. Just as everyone was accounted for and heading back to land, a huge wave broke over the top of them. The nurse handed Pierrepoint Jr. to the gardener, shouting, "Don't let water get in the baby's mouth!" In the next instant she was washed away. A lieutenant in the group swam after her, but he couldn't reach her. She was gone, and her body washed up later at Viking Beach.[15]

Newport's beaches and waterfront properties took a beating, including beloved Bailey's Beach, when the water crashed over the seawall, washing away buildings and docks and the fishing fleet, and demolishing a million dollars' worth of fish traps. But the loss of lives there was small compared to other communities in Narragansett Bay. Newport's fancier properties were often perched on higher land, and many of the grand houses were empty. Their summer occupants had already gone home to prepare for the fall social season in the cities.

XIII

The Narragansett Bay shoreline took the hurricane's hit squarely. Sustained winds of 121 miles per hour pushed up into the four-mile-wide mouth of Narragansett Bay, and the surge built to a height of fifty feet at certain points as it burst onto shore like the wrath of God coming in a wall of gray-blue water. Waiting at the head of the bay lay the city of Providence, where the square miles of surface water driven up by the wind from the bay's opening were funneled into a channel less than a mile wide. The water would find no place to go except into the heart of the city. The residents, like the Fogels and their wedding guests and the downtown business community, waited unsuspectingly to see when the weather would clear. A few were beginning to find the signs ominous, and to wonder what would happen next.

In the best of times the central waterfront was vulnerable to fluctuations in tides and weather. Downtown Providence was created by city fathers who extended the land and harbor to the utmost by building on marshland and filling in swamps at the head of the Providence River. Even city hall, located on Exchange Place, the city's hub, was set on wet clay, and at high tide water often flooded the basement. On September 21 the soil beneath the city was already water-logged from four days of rain that had soaked the ground and caused all the rivers and waterways to swell.

Providence was a Yankee town where American op-portunities and idealism reigned high in the public imagina-tion. Horatio Alger stories of rags-to-riches abounded as the town evolved from a seafaring capital to a paragon of Ameri-can industrialism. It was a port city whose citizenry welcomed the adventuresome and enterprising, from eighteenth-century sea captains to rumrunners during Prohibition. The city had been populated from the start by Catholics, Baptists, Jews, and Quakers who fled Massachusetts with Roger Williams to escape the Puritans. Its lively waterfront had helped it evolve from a center of the China trade during the nineteenth century to an emerging textile empire and bustling shipping center by the 1930s, by which time the overall population was a yeasty mix of Yankees, Irish, Italians, and Portuguese. The city was a leader of American industry in the early twentieth century, one of the richest industrial centers, with cutting-edge technologies. It was home to America's larg-est precision-tool factory, the largest file factory, the largest steam engine factory, and the largest silverware factory and screw factory. The convergence of Yankee ingenuity, immi-grant manpower, and waterfront geography set the stage for Providence's dominance of the mill and textile industry. It boasted the biggest textile manufacturer in the country, Fruit

of the Loom. However, by 1938 the Northeast textile industry had shown signs of yielding its lead to the South. In
addition, the Depression had put one-third of all workers
out of jobs in Providence.[16]

In fact Providence, like most of America, had lost a lot
of its shine by 1938. Social workers who handed out two-
dollar vouchers for doctor appointments and three-dollar-
a-week housing allowances to unemployed workers knew
how much desperation there was in the rooming houses and
tenements. The Depression had taken a big bite out of the
incomes and optimism of the city's poor. It had stolen their
prospects. It had also left them, desperate and deprived of
luxury and advantage, ever watchful and alert to chance.
As in most large cities of the time, but especially in mill towns
where thousands had been laid off, people locked their doors
and watched their purses.

The dire economy and general fretfulness fueled escap-
ist desires for fun and entertainment, and Providence offered
both. Singer and composer George M. Cohan of *Yankee
Doodle Dandy* fame was a native of Providence. A number of
splendid theaters were built between World War I and the
mid-thirties that hosted vaudeville, theater, musical revues,
and silent movies. By the time of the Depression, movies and
sports were the leading affordable attractions, and downtown movie theaters, like Loew's, were big and opulent.
Their deep carpets and glowing chandeliers were nearly the
only brush with luxury that Depression workers could enjoy.
People flocked downtown on the nickel trolley to soak up a
few hours of comfort and see whatever movie was playing
that week. Major downtown hotels hosted big bands and
regular dances for a young urban population that had mi-

grated from the countryside into the city as agriculture dwindled in much of the state. The Biltmore Hotel had been a hot spot since the Jazz Age a decade earlier and continued to lure patrons who could afford it for fun and glamour. Providence also exemplified the intense downtown focus that was typical of American cities before World War II. Department stores, theaters, restaurants, hotels, clubs — every active venue for a restless public was concentrated downtown.

It was ten minutes to three when meteorologist John Daily in the office of the U.S. Weather Bureau in Providence received the final telegram of the day from the Weather Bureau in Washington. It contained no hurricane warnings and advised that a tropical storm had been seventy-five miles southeast of Atlantic City, New Jersey, at noon. It was moving north-northeast, according to the report, and its center was expected to pass over Long Island or Connecticut late in the afternoon or early in the evening. The report was dutifully passed along to newspapers and radio stations.

David Patten at the *Providence Evening Bulletin* did not expect winds in Providence to exceed the 50 to 60 miles per hour predicted by an Associated Press dispatch from Washington at 3:30. But reports of high winds and fallen trees kept coming into the paper. The phones were ringing, and the reporters who came in from the street were wet and uneasy about conditions in the street. The weather was beginning to look like a big story for the Sports Extra edition. When a call came in about water rising in the street outside Ballan's downtown shoe store, he sent reporters there to see what the salesclerk who had phoned in was talking about. The reporters came back with their trouser legs rolled up, running for their typewriters. The harbor, they said, was washing into the city. It had reached Exchange Place, the center of town.

Patten and his employees looked out onto Fountain Street and saw a river of water starting at around the Biltmore Hotel and winding toward Union Street. The flood continued to rise and the wind increased, whipping it into whitecaps on the city streets. *Bulletin* staffers watched men and women creep along, the water up to their waists in some places, moving from one storefront or signpost to the next for support. Two women crouched next to the building on the street opposite of the paper and inched their way along, holding a little girl at shoulder height above the water. They could make little headway against the wind and were forced to hold onto the bricks of the building with their fingernails until a policeman came by and helped pull them along. Patten instructed the staff to keep back from the windows in case they blew in, but few obeyed. Everyone was so mesmerized by the scene on the street that they couldn't turn away. The wind sounded like thunder to him. He called his son Timmy, who was home alone, and advised him to batten down their house. Then he called his wife Marta, who was playing cards that afternoon in Rumstick Point. She laughed at her husband's concern. "Don't worry, I'm going home soon," she said.

More and more reporters returned to the office high on adrenaline. They complained about getting their shoes wet. Growing short of patience, Patten told them to get boots if they could, but to get going. "Get the story," he told them sharply. Shortly, a few men came back with stories to regale the newsroom. *You should see the town out there,* they said. A few whispered that they had just come across Pine Street where a car had been crushed by a tumbled wall. They had seen a body inside. A drowned man had been seen in Westminster Street, too.

Patten felt his nerves being stretched to the limit. "Saw, saw, saw," he chided the reporters for telling one another what they'd seen rather than getting down the story. "For God's sake, don't tell us, *write it!*" A newsman who much preferred accurate reporting to hyperbole, Patten could only describe the scene out his window as a nightmare. All his juices as a newsman were pumping. He called his reporter in West Warwick, Leonard Warner, who had already reported that big trees were falling in what looked like one incredible storm there. He told him to go to Westerly, where Patten had heard the storm was raging. The word hurricane had not yet slipped into his vocabulary. Patten knew he'd be in the office all night getting the paper ready to go to press the next morning.

Reporter Warner started out on his assignment to Westerly at about four o'clock. The wind made his small sedan skitter along the road. On Nooseneck Hill Road he blew all over the four-lane highway, unable to get his automobile under control. At one point it stood on its two right wheels, and luckily for Leonard it landed back down on all four tires instead of flipping over. But it was beyond Nooseneck Hill, when he spotted a chicken coop that had landed in the middle of the road, that he realized the storm's real danger. Over the brim of the hill was a traffic jam. As far as he could see, trees lay across the road. Those left standing continued to fall like soldiers on a field of battle. When he got out of the car to look at the situation, the boughs of a big tree arched overhead. He heard someone yell "Duck!" as the tree crashed behind him. He figured he would have to turn back, so he turned down a side road. As he rounded a sharp curve, a police car in front of him slammed on its brakes. Leonard did the same and the two cars spun together, landing side-by-side against a dirt embankment. It had happened so fast that Leonard had not seen that the police officer was avoiding a falling tree that surely would have killed the driver of any car it had struck. They were both stuck now, with no option but to hack at the tree, taking turns with the ax that the officer was carrying. They worked in the howling wind and rain, listening to the sound of other trees crashing in the vicinity. Finally they cleared enough of an area to drive through only moments before trees on both sides of the road were uprooted and blew over on the spot where they had stood. There was no way to get the story, or any warnings, to Providence.[17]

By now the residents of Providence were beginning to notice for themselves that the weather was worse than merely nasty. These days TV stations would monitor every twitch of the oncoming storm live from a "storm central" desk. But as the Great Hurricane bore down on Providence, there was remarkably little alarm even though it had devastated Long Island only two hours before. The radio stations were carrying only vague reports of a "tropical storm." The public was on its own. Schools let out, workers headed home, citizens decided on their own whether or not to go to the grocery store. As the storm struck, it pulled the plugs connecting citizens to their community. Telephones and electric power went quickly. With the power went radio. Chaos and paralysis spread.

When Robert Kenyon, twenty-three, went out on his lunch break in downtown Providence, it was rainy and blustery. He worked in advertising at Cherry & Webb, a women's specialty store in downtown Providence, and it was his job to walk over and place the store's newspaper advertisement at the office of the *Providence Journal,* three blocks away. He took his usual shortcut down a narrow side street that was protected from wind and rain, but still he could tell they were in for a big storm. Signs were blowing and squeaking in the wind on buildings all around him. When he reached the advertising desk of the newspaper office, a few people were grumbling about the weather. The sound of gravel blowing across the roof was mistaken for a hailstorm.

Downtown shoppers remarked on the worsening conditions all afternoon as they came and went in Cherry & Webb, but it wasn't until 4:30 that there was a ripple of news on everyone's tongue: downtown was flooding. The store manager called Robert down from his upper-floor office to the basement, where water was beginning to come into the store. He and the other employees heaped their arms full of low-end women's coats and fur-trimmed items to carry from the basement level up to the main floor just as water started coming through the side doors of the store. Within minutes the water was hip-high in the basement. Robert cringed when he saw a rat swimming in with the floodwater. He dumped the coats on a dry counter and went back downstairs for another armload only to discover that the transom windows between the street level and the basement had blown in from the water pressure, and that water was now cascading into the basement like a waterfall. There was nothing that he or the other fifty employees could do except rush for the ground floor. They looked speechlessly at one another. They had never seen a storm like this and they couldn't believe it. In half an hour the lights went out and the five-story department store went dark. Water was standing two feet deep on the ground floor and still rising.

The hurricane had hit Providence with full force slightly after four. The surge poured upward over the seawall and filled the streets. Water rose eighteen feet above the low tide level across the three-mile business and industrial district between three and six o'clock. At five o'clock, waves and surges topped the ramparts of the Providence River in the heart of town, and the water rose six feet in the downtown area within thirty minutes.[18] Thousands were marooned on the upper floors of banking and business offices. Workers looked down from upper-floor offices onto a scene more like Venice than New England. Some people took refuge on the steps of city hall, hoping the water wouldn't rise that high. The exclusive all-male Hope Club next door allowed women through its doors for the first time in history.

With phone lines out, word of the flooding downtown spread slowly, but the storm's ferocity became evident in every part of the city. Incredulity was the typical reaction. "Do you often have storms like this in Rhode Island?" asked a girl from out of state at the freshman afternoon tea at Pembroke College (now part of Brown University) on the east side of Providence.

St. Xavier's Academy dismissed its students at 2:30 because of the storm. Three high school girls, age fifteen, started home together. The wind was so high that they had to grab a phone pole to keep from being blown down the street. They stopped into a nearby cafeteria to get out of the wind. No sooner were they settled inside than a woman was blown through the front plate glass window. Her hand was badly cut and blood seemed to spew everywhere. The girls were aghast. They huddled in the cafeteria waiting for the storm to end, growing increasingly uneasy. One gathered her rosary beads out of her book bag. When water began coming in under the cafeteria door, the girls followed the other patrons up the stairs toward an overhead bakery. The door was locked when they got there, but the men in the group broke it down. A few others began going up the fire escape. As the chairs on the ground floor started floating, panic seized the patrons below and one man began to stampede over the others to get up the fire escape. In a scuffle that followed, he was thrown back down the stairs. The girls felt safer on the second floor, but they knew they were stranded under bewildering circumstances. They were also starved, so they helped themselves to an apple pie off the baker's shelf and ate it with their fingers.

There was a certain irony in the storm for F. van Wyck Mason, a novelist and historian who had fled to Providence to get out of the rain and in the end found himself literally in the eye of the storm. Mason had a summer home in Nantucket, and that summer he had stayed late and completed a seven-hundred-page manuscript of a novel he had been writing for the previous eighteen months. He was traveling to New York City to deliver it to his publisher. The first leg of his trip was between Nantucket and New Bedford by ferry. The trip was miserable, and if the high waves and seasick passengers weren't trial enough, the steamboat ferry, assaulted by the wind and high seas, crashed into a pier. Mason was anxious to get to the safety of a train or plane to finish his trip, but the only way out of New Bedford in such weather was by bus. He was also making every effort to keep his manuscript dry. It was safely locked in his briefcase. He caught a bus to Providence, figuring that he could make better connections to New York from there. He arrived nearly at the moment the hurricane struck the city, and as he climbed off the bus, bricks off a nearby chimney showered the street in front of his feet. He held the briefcase with his manuscript in it above his head for protection from falling objects and rushed for the train station. As he watched the water rise ten feet in the square below the station, he began to realize that conditions were far more than an obstacle course between him and getting to New York. A full-fledged disaster was upon Providence. He stood in horror as a woman drowned trying to climb out of her sinking car and another, seemingly wading to safety, suddenly dropped out of sight. He was badly shaken, and he knew there was no way out of Providence that night. So he made his way to the Hope Club for the night and sat up by candlelight with his manuscript safely on his lap.[19]

In downtown Providence the situation became more dramatic as the afternoon wore on. Frederick Williamson worked for Baird North on Orange Street, the largest mail-order jewelry business in the country. As the most junior staff member, he helped with everything from shipping to repairs. It was never mentioned that he was the only black man in the store, and at the end of each day he returned to Providence's north end, where there was a vibrant black community. He was unable to eat out in the downtown restaurants or go to the city's clubs for entertainment, so his after-hours life, like most black people's at the time, was centered around church events. But during the day he enjoyed being downtown and feeling part of the commercial hustle that was Providence's thriving jewelry business. The city boasted the largest jewelry manufacturing business in the country.

By mid-afternoon Williamson wanted to see what was going on outside. He and the other employees could hear the marquees rattling in the wind and see passersby hunkering down as they rushed down the street. He'd had a sense all day that something ominous was coming in the weather. He walked down to Exchange Place to get a look at the sky. The wide expanse across from city hall was the terminus for all the city's buses and streetcars and the best place to judge the weather. It was hard to see the sky from the often dark and narrow downtown streets in the commercial district. That day he could feel the tension in the air as shoppers hurried to get home in the high wind and increasing rain.

When he returned to the store, he told his coworkers that the weather looked bad and that he didn't think the store could stay open. He was worried that the big new display windows in the front of the store would blow in. The water was already rising up Orange Street.

The store manager asked him to usher the four woman employees to the upper floors of the building, and with the water starting to rise in the streets outside, Frederick knew that the best way to avoid having to go outdoors was to guide

them through the furnace room in the basement and up into
the building's main lobby. On his way back he passed the
shipping department, also downstairs, and saw that the street-
level water was beginning to pour into the basement. The
sight added to his sense of approaching disaster. The store
manager asked him to move quickly to help him bring in all
the fine jewelry and gems on display in the windows. The
staff was cautious about leaving jewelry in the windows
overnight anyhow, but the added risk of the windows being
blown in made Frederick and the manager work urgently
to get everything out of sight and put away. The safe, where
the jewels were stored, looked heavy enough to survive a
flood. The water in the furnace room and the torrent rising
over the curb in the street suggested that that was what they
were in for. Once the remaining staff of men had stored the
jewels and emptied the till, they turned their attention to the
street. The water was getting higher and they could see that
it had now risen several feet up the double glass front doors.
They could no longer open the doors against the pressure.
Frederick went back to look at the furnace room, but it was
completely flooded. They looked up at the transom windows
overhead at the front of the store and considered them to be
their only hope for escape. With a ladder from the stockroom,
Frederick climbed up. The others handed him up some of
the jeweler's tools so he could break the windows. Then, one
at a time, they climbed up and dropped down into the water
outside.

On the sidewalk they could barely keep their footing
in the rushing water. Baird North's newly remodeled storefront provided no moldings or decorative exterior that could
offer them a handhold. People on the floors above saw their

predicament and threw several ropes out the window so they might haul themselves up, but the blowing wind held the ropes out from the building, rippling and waving beyond their reach. They knew they were in trouble. A few store-fronts down the street, they could see another group of men, slightly better positioned to avoid the current, anxiously watching their progress.

Then, bumping toward them in the current came a railroad tie that had apparently broken loose down at the harbor. Both groups of men watched it approach. The street was like a river. The other men seemed to decide that Frederick and his colleagues were most at risk; when the log came their way, they gave it a shove toward Frederick's group downstream. The water was now up to his chest. A man of moderately slight build at five-foot-seven, he asked the others to keep hold of him as he reached out toward the tie. Once he had it firmly in his arms, all five men grabbed on. It was awkward and unwieldy in the swirling current, like a wild horse that wants to go its own way, thought Frederick. There was only a second to jump on and drift out in the continually rising and fast-moving water.

The water was now climbing up several main down-town arteries. It came from the bay on one side up Orange Street and also up Fawcett, then met at an intersecion in front of the New England Market. The convergence was like a horror-film sequence in which the hero sees menace coming from one direction and reverses his course only to find the same threat coming at him from the other way, too. The waters at the juncture between Orange and Fawcett swirled like a whirlpool as they deepened and pushed the men sideways up Weybosset Street, further uptown. The scene was so bizarre that the men on the railroad tie were speechless. They could hardly have been heard over the sound of the wind and water anyhow. No one commented until they floated past the spot where one of Frederick's coworkers had parked his car behind the Baird North store. Only its top was visible above the water. The owner moaned audibly from his end of the tie as they floated past. "I loved that car," they heard him say. The streets had become canals, and the men had no control over where the rushing water would take them. The current was gaining speed, rising up into the city and getting deeper at the same time. It wasn't high tide quite yet.

When the log hit the corner in front of the Dorrance Building, the five jumped off and ran up the wide stairs to the building's second floor to get above the water level. Many people from the building and off the street had congregated there. Frederick recognized several of the elevator operators, fellow black men from his home neighborhood, who were busily working to pull people in off the street through the second-story windows, now at water-height. Everyone was wet and wrapped in whatever coats and blankets they could come by. They looked relieved, but pathetic.

The storm was at its worst when thousands started home at five o'clock. As downtown workers poured into Exchange Place to catch the trolleys and buses that would take them home, the hurricane, like a performer waiting for the audience to arrive and take their seats before raising the curtain, unleashed its full strength and fury. Winds of 100 miles per hour whipped through the streets. High tide, just before six o'clock, shoved eight to ten additional feet of water into the downtown maze of streets and avenues at roughly the same time. Chimneys began to blow off buildings. As the reporters from the *Providence Journal* had begun to see, there were drownings and other casualties. Corpses washed by in the street and a few could be seen lying under fallen debris. Few bystanders could do anything to help. In order to save themselves, they had to climb higher up in buildings just to stay a few steps ahead of the surging aquarium out in the streets as the water, full of menace now, licked at their heels. The open air was no safer. Glass shards rained from dozens of blown-out windows. Signs and marquees ripped from buildings whirled through the air and crashed. Power lines dangled, sparked, and blew in the wind like a circus master's whip.

Chaos and disorder gave rise to an air of otherworldliness as communications failed. Public awareness of events was varied, disjointed, and filtered through the emotional scrim of shock. Several hundred people taking refuge in the lobby of a downtown building did not know the gravity of the situation until a band of survivors arrived, swimming. Amused by the sight of the dripping newcomers, the crowd tittered until it became evident that one woman in the party was bleeding and might be near death. The tragedy was more than most people could wrap their minds around. It was serious, deadly, and within an hour's time, hard upon them. Rising water flooded power and transmission stations after the wind had knocked out all the transmission lines anyhow. Without phones or radio to connect them, each group felt isolated in its struggle to survive.

All over the city, mothers and wives at home waited to hear from children and husbands who went to school and worked downtown. They did not know the extent of the calamity. At six o'clock the number of people sheltered in city hall stood at five hundred, and the water was still rising. As darkness fell on the city, stranded office workers, now without power and light, watched helplessly as pedestrians below floated past in the currents. The mayor declared an emergency curfew to prevent more looting and protect the public.

The scene in the street was eerie as darkness fell. Car horns blared underwater and some headlights shone like underwater lights in a swimming pool. Rats, refrigerators, and department store mannequins floated next to people plastered up against doorways or swimming for their lives alongside the debris.

Then, just after dark, a shadowy element emerged. Looters came swimming, holding flashlights out of the water over their heads. They entered the broken, washed-out windows of the department stores. Onlookers watched from floors above as the first few appeared. Among the observers was the writer David De Jong, who would describe the scene for *Yankee* magazine. "They seemed organized, almost regimented, as if they'd daily drilled and prepared for this event, the like of which hadn't happened in a hundred and twenty years. They were brazen and insatiable; they swarmed like rats, they took everything." It was the opportunity so many had waited for, to finally have some of what they had been missing through those long Depression years. Policemen came around to patrol in a motorboat, but they couldn't stop them. The looters outnumbered the officers, who were more intent on rescue than law enforcement at the moment. It is also possible that some just decided to look away rather than pick a fight and have to stare into the ravenous determination on the looters' faces.

Whitecaps now flooded the Fountain Street offices of the *Providence Evening Bulletin*. With the power out, some reporters stayed in the newsroom and worked under lanterns and flashlights. Others escaped holding typewritten copy over their heads to keep it dry. Things weren't going any better for workers at the *Providence Journal,* whose printing plant was damaged by the flood. A few of the staffers remarked wryly among themselves that the final edition of the *Journal* had gone out on the morning of the twenty-first reading, "Heavy rain this afternoon and tonight—fair and cooler tomorrow."

Fortunately, Robert Kenyon in the Cherry & Webb department store had parked his Pontiac coupe on high ground. It was his first car, and he thanked his stars that he hadn't parked in the waterfront parking down on the town docks. Those cars were now all afloat, like large turtles in the city street. The sound of shorted car horns gave him the creeps. The scene was unbelievable to him. A drive that typically took him fifteen minutes consumed several hours as he navigated by trial and error around streets that were flooded or, up on high ground, blocked by fallen trees. He couldn't wait to get home and wash his hair after the cascade of street water that had poured in on him. When he finally arrived home at his parents' house on Larsen Street, his mother had no idea what state the downtown was in. She had not heard from his father, who also worked downtown. She also didn't realize that the phone lines were out.

One of the girls who had been at the Pembroke College tea picked her way home in total darkness to Keene Street, where she lived with her aunt. So many trees were blown down on campus that those students who lived off campus had to climb carefully around them in order to get home, guided by Boy Scout volunteers with flashlights after dark. She worried the whole way that she might not find the house standing until she spied the candle burning in the window of the upstairs sitting room as she approached.

Meanwhile, the Fogel family across town in the Elmhurst section of Providence began to make its way downtown for their son's wedding. What was typically a ten-minute drive from their home to the center of Providence took more than an hour. There were so many trees down in Elmwood that Josef Sr. had to wind around on side streets to find an open route. The water was already rising downtown, but it seemed preposterous to Josef, his wife, and mother-in-law that it could be a result of the storm. They assumed that a water main had broken until a policeman at one of the intersections screamed urgently at them from across the street, "Get up to Union Station!" Mrs. Fogel panicked. "We're going home!" she ordered her husband, but he countered her quietly: "We're going to Union Station." The station was located on a rise, well above the harbor. While the father went to park the car, Josef the groom, his sister Marilyn, and his mother and grandmother went inside the station to keep dry. Marilyn had on her silver slippers and semiformal long dress, and the rest of her family was wearing their wedding finery as well. They looked a bit incongruous alongside the rest of the people looking for refuge as they settled onto the hard seats in Union Station. When her father returned from parking the car in front of the station, he stopped at a newsstand and bought oranges and candy in case they were going to be stuck for a while. Word traveled through the station that the skylight ceiling of the Providence Public Library, a source of great civic pride, had crashed.

The seriousness of the situation began to dawn on them when the electricity went out and trucks outside the station pulled up and shone their lights so the interior would not be in total darkness. Josef wanted to call his bride Lorraine and explain the situation, but the phones were out as well. There was no way to reach her and the wedding guests at the Narragansett Hotel, so they settled down to wait. The excitement and tension made Marilyn, fourteen, fidgety. She made many trips to the ladies room until the little windows over the lavatory sinks crashed in from the wind and rain. Her father ushered her to a spot in the overhang of the station roof where she could relieve herself, though she felt funny about doing it in her good party clothes.

As night fell, they began to see evidence of what was going on down in the city center. Looters were coming through the train station, some of them carrying bottles of liquor. It was almost 11:00 P.M. when they heard that the water downtown was starting to recede, and the National Guard arrived to ask everyone to leave in an effort to control the area and keep the looters away from the station. The city was a wartime specter without electricity or lights. The mayor had declared a state of emergency by then and posted searchlights around the downtown area. Soldiers were patrolling the business district.

Josef Fogel Sr., followed by his family on foot, led the quarter-mile walk downhill to the Narragansett Hotel. Marilyn's silver slippers were thoroughly wet when they got there, but she forgot all about them when they entered the hotel and the waiting crowd cheered. Though some wedding guests had not made it, dozens of uninvited people had come into the hotel from the street, eaten the food, and drunk the champagne. Women in the wedding party screamed with delight that the groom and his family were there at last. Judge Maurice Robinson, anxious to get home to his own family, had waited. The bride and groom and guests were promptly hustled into one of the hotel rooms off the mezzanine, where the judge performed the ceremony then quickly left. Against the odds, the bride and groom's families tried to salvage an atmosphere of celebration. They returned to the main dining room, where the food had been eaten up, but Josef Fogel produced a bottle of liquor from the hotel staff and poured a round of drinks. The guests from Boston were concerned with the fate of their cars in the waters below, but the newlyweds were lucky. Joseph's 1937 Plymouth convertible with the rumble seat, planned as their getaway car, was parked on the second level of the hotel garage. Still, there was no way they could get the car that night. The National Guard came to their rescue when Josef Sr. slipped them a word, and with bayonets raised they escorted the newly married couple several blocks down the street to the Biltmore Hotel for their wedding night. As Josef and Lorraine registered as man and wife, they were given a candle to light their way to their room. The rest of the party stayed behind at the Narragansett and settled in for the night. Every room and easy chair seemed to be taken, so the Fogel family scrounged around for dining chairs and pulled them together enough to curl up on. Marilyn could not go to sleep. She heard gunshots during the night as the police and National Guard fired on looters. An announcement was made over megaphones on the street that looters would be shot, yet she watched people carry fur coats out of neighboring department stores and scurry down the street. Sofas washed out of furniture stores and spun down the avenues. Manhole covers burst. Model T's and A's bobbed along the streets of water.

Two sources of light shone in the dark. One was a pinkish glow from the southern sky where New London, Connecticut, was burning. People guessed there was a fire but they didn't know where, and the thought of fire made them uneasy. There were no phones to call for assistance, no streets that a fire truck could travel.

The other glimmer of light came from the offices of the *Providence Bulletin*. While his staff toiled by candle, lantern, and flashlight above, David Patten went to the basement with a flashlight to see what condition the presses were in. One hundred tons of newsprint had swelled in the water and burst out of its rolls. The presses' alarm bells were ringing and, ironically, the sprinkler pipes were sprinkling, haywire like everything else. Fish swam in the inky water. The presses were underwater along with the transformers and electrical controls for the building. Patten saw that he could not publish from Providence. He decided to call the publisher of the *Boston Post* as soon as the first phone line came back into service to see if he could publish the Providence paper from Boston.

Wind and water were the primary weapons in the hurricane's arsenal, but they let loose other demons of destruction on land. Connecticut, like western Massachusetts, was already waterlogged after unseasonably high rainfall. Eleven to seventeen inches had fallen during the previous four days. Area rivers were swollen, and the soil was damp to the roots of its oldest trees before the hurricane even reached Long Island Sound. The damage came in stages, first tearing at docks and wharves and driving boats disastrously ashore as it had all along the coast. Even the massive three-hundred-foot-long training ship of the American Nautical Academy, the *Marsala,* in New London, was driven aground like a toy despite a total of 1,220 feet of mooring chain and eighteen tons of anchor. Trees toppled and piers shattered under the assault.

The fire in the sky that the Moores had seen from Barn Island that night was the New London blaze, which was visible from Providence. It had begun at 4:30 when water flooded the building of a large wholesale grocer and short-circuited the wiring. This caused fire to break out in the city's business district, and the blaze fanned out within minutes. The situation was desperate almost from the start. Firemen called to the site could not reach it because fallen trees so completely blocked their path. The time it took to hack them out of the way cost precious minutes, until more than a dozen commercial buildings had caught fire. Fire departments in neighboring towns could not be summoned because all the phone lines were down. Those who did answer distress calls on the few existing shortwave radios, like those in the Oswegatchie and Waterford firehouses, found the roads so thoroughly blocked with fallen trees and phone lines that they had to turn back. The firefighters were stunned and frustrated by the brilliant blaze ahead of them in the night sky. It was visible from fifty miles away, but they could not reach it.

The high winds whipped the fire into an inferno that incinerated the furniture companies, grain stores, factories, office buildings, and lumberyards in New London's richest commercial area. The diminishing rain was not enough to quench it, but had the earlier torrent not soaked the buildings, the damage would have been worse. The wind was strong enough to blow the water streams from the fire hoses back into the firefighters' faces. Not since Benedict Arnold had burned New London for the British in the Revolutionary War had such an all-out disaster swept through town. And then the wind shifted. The change was capricious; it merely changed the streets that would be lost. Roofs were afire on Tilley Street, but the shift in wind direction saved that block and several adjoining streets from total destruction even though the damage wasn't over yet. Another store with a huge stock of furniture lay in the fire's new path and was consumed. After six and a half hours of mostly futile struggle, Fire Chief Thomas Shipman prepared to dynamite buildings in the path of the fire rather than let it reduce the entire town to ashes. Mercifully, as his men readied the blast, the wind shifted again. The fire was pushed back the way it had come over an already blackened path of ashes that was wet from the rain. By 2:00 A.M. the fire was under control, still smoldering and steaming in the wetness. New London would survive, but a quarter square mile of its richest commercial district, containing fourteen of the city's principal businesses, had gone up in smoke.[20]

❋ ❋ ❋

It was well after dark when the Cleaveland phone rang in Springfield, Massachusetts. The ringing startled Jean and her father, who assumed that the phone service was still out. Jean answered. "Are you Jean?" the caller asked. It was the shopkeeper in Noank where Polly Cleaveland and Fanny Hebert had shopped that afternoon. She told Jean that she had sold a footstool to her mother earlier in the day. The woman hesitated and drew a breath. "My husband is the undertaker here," she said, and went on to explain that many bodies had been brought into the funeral parlor following the storm. The shopkeeper had recognized Polly and Fanny immediately. Polly had put her phone number on her check. The shopkeeper knew where to call.

❋ ❋ ❋

Planes passed over Barn Island during the night, and as each one approached the Moore family, they yelled and waved, but to no avail. The hay and the insects it harbored caused them all to scratch and complain, but it kept them warm. The girls heard the sound of little animals scurrying beneath them in the hay. Catherine told them to not worry, that the critters were probably squirrels, though she knew, and Anne, the eldest, suspected, that they were sleeping with rats. Jim Nestor was still wearing just his underwear, and all the women had stripped down to their slips and undergarments before they were set afloat so their clothing wouldn't weigh them down in the water. Overnight they huddled together and slept the best they could.

XIV

As quickly as the storm had arrived, it departed, its waste laid all across the cities and shorefront in its wake. The effect of its wrath continued to be felt as inland rivers rose, and its very exit flourish north into New Hampshire was made with 160 mile per hour gusts that downed trees and continued to batter homes and property.[21] But the big cat had thrown its last wild tantrum and, like real cats do, suddenly gained its footing and leapt out of sight with a final hiss. Decelerating, it reached Burlington, Vermont, by 9:00 P.M. Suddenly the pandemonium on the coast was over. Despite the hurricane's colossal and dramatic arrival on the shorefront, landfall was its undoing. Its powers began to wane as it could no longer draw moisture from the ocean. Denied the sea-surface cycle of evaporation and water vapor required to feed its engine, it sputtered and died. By the time the Great Hurricane reached Canada the next morning, it was prancing along at a mere 50 miles per hour, trailing rain squalls.

* * *

Dawn broke on the East Coast as pristine and splendidly as ever. Its fresh beauty suggested for a fairy-tale instant that perhaps the whole ugly ordeal had been only a bad dream. The air seemed to glisten and the sky was blue and cloudless, with barely a ripple of wind. It was the kind of day when people often thought about going to the beach.

Shortly after sunrise on Long Island, Stuart Vorpahl traveled from Amagansett to Montauk in a big truck he had managed to appropriate. The water had receded enough to allow a big vehicle to pass through the shallow points between the towns without being submerged. But the Montauk he arrived at looked vastly different from the one he had known before the storm. Roads were washed away and houses were gone or nearly demolished along the shore. It looked as if the whole area had been furiously combed until every growing thing was hanging only by its roots or upended, and what remained had been tossed about. The sight made his heart race, and he hurried to the store and office, looking for Helen. He found her at the Duryea house. Helen threw her arms around him and told him she was worried about her mother and father and little brother. When Stuart told her that he had heard they had escaped by train and were safe in the Montauk Manor, she relaxed into his arms. At last she could let down. They climbed into the truck and Stuart drove her to her family, and then they all went back to the Vorpahl house in Amagansett, which was still standing. The Bengston house was unlivable, but it was one of the few that remained standing on the beach. The next day in

New York's *Daily News,* Helen's grandmother's house, also in Amagansett, was featured in a photograph. The house, lifted away and floated toward the railroad tracks, was nothing but kindling when it got there. All that was left standing was a toilet, now out in the open. It and a little washbasin had been added to the porch some years back when indoor plumbing became the norm.

* * *

Amid the grief and sorrow of loss, there were numerous instances of mistaken reports and happy reunions. In Westhampton on Long Island, Norvin Greene, whose efforts to find his wife Tot, their children, and a houseful of guests — first by car, then by boat and even a Coast Guard escort vessel — had been thwarted at every turn. By Thursday morning he and a friend had gotten the boat out of the boathouse where their car windshield had been smashed the night before. They approached the dunes and soon spotted a small band of people moving toward the bay. A crippled man was being carried on a door and there was a small child in the party. One of the men with Norvin felt obliged to rescue this pathetic-looking group first, and Norvin was nearing the end of his patience. His anxiety over the fate of his family was nearly unendurable. But he managed to wait until the crippled man and child had been taken back to the mainland so he could resume his search.

When he set out in the boat seeking his family again, he saw only empty dunes where houses near his own had stood. Of 179 houses between Shinnecock Bay and Moriches Inlet before the storm, only 25 were still standing. Disoriented by the changes in the dunes and landscape made by the storm, he barely recognized his own house when he first saw it. The hurricane had actually rearranged the shoreline and surface of the land like a sculptor shaping clay. The docks were gone. He and his companion jumped out of the boat at the spot where they had once stood and began wading to a group of survivors coming toward them on the beach. Tot, Norvin's wife, his children Gair and Gretchen, and Patricia Bradley were among them. There was hardly time to revel in the moment with so many others to help.

❊ ❊ ❊

Anyone who had a boat and a truck at their disposal had driven to the shore overnight to join the rescue effort. The New York City Coast Guard had also come, but the amount of wreckage and downed telephone and electrical wires made the job of search and rescue hazardous and overwhelming. Otis Bradley rescued his children Otis and Margaret, and took Patricia Driver with him in a small boat belonging to the harbormaster. When the Greenes reached the dockside of Westhampton Beach, they heard a Lowell Thomas radio broadcast reporting that Mrs. Norvin Greene, her two children, and guests had all been drowned at sea, with their million-dollar mansion destroyed as well. But their momentary amusement was tempered by others' losses. Ned Lea, who had searched the night before with Norvin for his family, did not find his wife's body until several days later.

What the news media had missed in real-time reporting they made up for in sensationalized coverage after the fact. The same radio report that declared the death of the Greene family announced that Westhampton had been wiped off the face of the earth, causing serious distress to distant families of Westhampton residents. Listening in Brooklyn, where she had gone to visit her family, was the mother of an eighteen-year-old boy who had ridden out the storm in Westhampton. She went into shock and mourning, only to learn a day later that her son had survived.

* * *

Later that day, Long Island was abuzz with news about fishermen who were lost in the storm. The two brothers whom Helen had overheard in the store debating whether or not to move their boat had apparently started out too late to get it to safety. They were caught asea by the peak of the storm and drowned. Another fishing boat, one of those that Stevie Dellapolla had watched going out when his own captain had made the decision to return to port, had continued to Gardiners Island to lift its fish traps and vanished. Four men were on the boat; only the captain's body was found.

The worst news was that the Smith Meal Company's bunker steamer *Ocean View*, which had sailed out of the Promised Land fish factory dock, was lost. It had turned back east for Promised Land, into the wind and seas, and was making progress until the boat's crankshaft broke and the doors blew off the engine room. Water poured into the wallowing boat. The captain ordered the men into two of the seine boats that the steamer carried. He and sixteen men took one and six took the other. The second boat, manned entirely by the blacks of the crew, capsized getting away from the larger boat and all six men drowned. The captain and the other sixteen men blew ten miles across Long Island Sound to Madison, Connecticut, where their boat was hurled ashore over a concrete seawall close to midnight. News of their survival did not reach Montauk until the following night.

The *Robert E.*, another bunker boat with Stevie Dellapolla's brother-in-law on board, had gone out at the same time as the *Ocean View*. When the weather worsened, the captain of the *Robert E.* decided to not turn back into the wind. He headed northwest toward New Haven on the Connecticut coast and ran with the following seas for over an hour. As he approached the harbor, he could see no buoys, and the water was so high they could not spot the ten-foot-high breakwater. Somehow—over or around the breakwater—they ended up in the harbor, and the captain safely grounded the *Robert E.* on the flats.

For several days after the hurricane, there were sightings of boats presumed lost and the arrival of thankful, shaken crews that seemed risen from the dead for the families who awaited word of them. There were also wrecks and bodies that washed ashore and a few others that had vanished without a trace.

As people emerged from what shelter they had managed to find when the storm struck, they began to realize the scope of the disaster. Hardly a household or soul was untouched either by death, destruction, or trauma. Whole towns and those who lived in them were in shock. It wasn't that a large, vague, dreadful thing had happened, but always something terribly specific. There were thousands and thousands of quite specific tragedies—a home lost, a death, a community destroyed. It was a huge pattern of very individual occurrences, like the two boys, Charles Lucas, twenty, and Tommy Fay, twenty-one, who had risked their lives for a hundred-dollar offer to rescue a Westhampton resident's dogs. Their bodies were washed ashore in Hampton Bays six days after the storm.

❋ ❋ ❋

Inland on the Hendrickson chicken farm, the damage was almost more than Rick could assimilate. All twenty-six of the chicken houses were razed, and there was not one of his one thousand hens to be seen. Only the water pipes for the automatic drinking fountains for the birds remained. The new Johns Manville slate shingles had blown off the farmhouse. His wife Dorothea finally appeared after dark, bruised and dirtied. She had managed to get out of Southampton with their Model A roadster, but so many trees had been down when she reached Bridgehampton that she had abandoned the car and walked the rest of the way, frequently climbing to get over fallen trees in her path.

The damage to the farm and the chicken flock demoralized Rick, but he did not have time to wallow in his distress. Thirty cows had to be milked by flashlight that night, and the next morning he had to take the milk to another dairy in Southampton that was badly damaged. With windows and doors to fix, there was enough, he reflected, to keep him busy from the moment he got up until he fell asleep at day's end for as long as he could see ahead.

❋ ❋ ❋

At Grassmere in Southampton, the Lee family had weathered the hurricane without incident. The water had risen from Lake Agawam as high as the porch and stayed there, lapping at the house for the duration of the storm, but at no time did the family members think of evacuating. However, there was much anxiety over the Irish maid Sheila, who had taken two small boys, Lee's cousin and his friend, on an outing. The boys had grown restless in the house reading The Green Hornet, Superman, and The Shadow comic books during the overcast morning, so Sheila had taken them out after lunch. No one was quite sure where they had gone. They had, in fact, gone to the beach, but Sheila, always cautious about the children, had become alarmed by the weather and rising water sooner than the other beachcombers and dragged the two eight-year-olds across the Meadow Club tennis courts before the surge carried the courts and most of the club across the road. They had waited out the worst of the weather on the roof of an extended family member's beach house until the Coast Guard rescued them. They were lucky. Sheila had tried to call Grassmere so the family wouldn't worry, but all phones were out of service.

The Lee grandchildren would never forget an event that occurred on Grassmere's front lawn the next morning. Furnishings of all sorts that had been washed out of homes and clubs on the shoreline had floated and blown up from the lake. All the children turned out in the sunny morning to see what "treasures" had washed up on their lawn. Their grandmother was determined to identify the pieces and return them to their rightful owners. She and the servants set them up to dry and looked them over for details that might help identify their owners. One bureaulike chest was from the beach club. It contained the chits that club members

signed when they bought drinks at the bar. Their grandmother opened the accounts drawer and saw that many were
assigned to her husband, who had told her that he had given
up drinking. At least he was never seen drinking at home
anymore. She drew herself up and called into the house:
"Jim, why do you lie to me and tell me you are not drinking?" There was a sly twinkle behind her stern expression.

XV

Tragedy and comedy mixed incongruously in the aftermath of the storm, and survivors emerged from the ordeal with displays of heart and spirit.

On the Connecticut coast, the Hepburn house in Fenwick was gone when Katharine and her friend Red Hammond rose at dawn the next morning and went to see the damage. It had floated a third of a mile downstream before getting stuck on a stone bridge near the opening of the Connecticut River. Her brother had looked back the previous afternoon and watched it sail down the swamp. With Hepburn spirit, the family resolved to build again. Katharine and Red began to dig in the ruins and recovered eighty-five pieces of silverware and the household tea service. Kate, always the movie star, posed among the rubble in a clawfoot bathtub for a photo with Red alongside, looking at her adoringly while seated on a toilet.

Emily Fowler in Old Lyme, Connecticut, had been rescued after floating ashore in the squatters' colony at the mouth of Black Hall. Her boyfriend Atwood, who had gone ashore for help after being separated from Emily and their sailboat, had formed a search party to look for her. The family's friend and physician, Dr. Griswold, was among those who found her at ten that night. She had spent four hours in the water. Dr. Griswold told Emily that he had seen her mother that afternoon in Essex, where she had taken Emily's younger sister and friends to the movies. She had been headed down to Saybrook to look for Emily's body. While Emily was fed supper in a farmhouse along the water that was taking in refugees, the rescue party went on to help others, but Dr. Griswold was able to reach Emily's mother with the news that her daughter was safe. But awkwardly enough, the word did not reach Emily's younger sister, Franny. When Emily ran into Franny the following day in the drugstore in Old Lyme, Franny was wearing one of her sister's favorite skirts and a sweater. Emily, amazed, unleashed one of her most withering big-sister looks. "But I thought you were dead," Franny explained lamely.

※ ※ ※

Two days after the hurricane, a salvage and rescue worker brought the footstool that Polly Cleaveland had bought the day she drowned back into the Noank shop where she purchased it. It had been recovered with the shop tag still tied to its dainty upturned foot. This time the shopkeeper was glad to call Polly's daughter Jean, in Springfield. It was easier to be the bearer of good news. She phoned to say that she had the engagement present that Polly had intended for her daughter. It had been found in Polly's car, submerged two hundred feet off the road in marsh waters where police troopers had swum to recover the bodies. A delivery truck driver told the state police that he had seen their car parked near a sandbar minutes before the surge. He told the women they weren't safe there and urged them to leave with him and climb to higher ground on foot, but they had refused. The driver had moved on alone.

Adams Nickerson got back to St. Mark's School in Southborough, Massachusetts, by midafternoon on September 22. The morning after the hurricane, he started walking with his bags for the bus stop, two miles away. He felt lucky when a driver offered him a lift. When he reached Westerly by bus, he learned there were no more trains coming through for Boston, so the bus driver took his passengers to Providence. From there Adams and some of his fellow students caught a bus to Boston. They changed to yet another bus for Southborough, which ran out of gas on the last leg of their journey. Adams and several other boys who had been on The Bostonian the day of the hurricane wrote about their experiences in *The Vindex,* the St. Mark's student journal. His two classmates wrote of being soaked to the bone, and one told of trying to swim ashore still wearing his overcoat. Only Adams managed to keep his new suit dry. "And so at last I arrived," he wrote. "It had taken us twenty-six hours to get from New York to Southborough — the most extraordinary journey I have ever had."

Rhode Island reeled from the devastation the hurricane left behind. In Westerly the Reverend G. Edgar Tobin lived out what he told his son Jack was the most trying period of his life. As the local high school became the town morgue,

hearses lined up where the school buses had stopped before, and the town's five undertakers ran out of embalm-
ing fluid. The hurricane killed two hundred in Westerly.
The firehouse whistle was blown every time a body was
found. Tobin performed back-to-back funerals over the next
few days, some doubled, with mother and child buried together in the same coffin. He officiated over each of the
funerals for the women of the Christ Episcopal Church
Mothers' Club. The church bells tolled mournfully all day.

Around Westerly they told the tale of a woman who
was in a newly built beach house with a massive granite fireplace anchored with steel rods. She felt safe enough to go
up to the third floor and watch the storm when the waves
rose above the first-story windows. An eighteen-foot rise in
tide chased her up to the windowless attic, where she started
feeling nauseous and groggy enough to fall asleep. Her son
and husband found her on the land side of the barrier pond
the next morning, where the entire third floor had washed
up like a boat. When she told them her story, they realized
that her nausea had been seasickness. She arrived ashore
rested and completely ignorant of the prior evening's events,
or so she said.

※ ※ ※

A nineteen-year-old boy went out cruising in his car in
Watch Hill after the storm to see the extent of the storm
and offer help to those who needed it. He found a friend,
a girl he knew from his church choir, completely naked
along the road. She had broken her leg, and the wind and
water had stripped her clothes off. Though they continued

to sing together at church, they never spoke of the incident again.

* * *

The dimensions of the disaster on the coastline were harder for city residents to grasp. Some drove down to the shore to see what had happened for themselves, though the declaration of martial law in many areas to prevent looters, the number of fallen trees and other obstacles across the roads, and washed-out bridges and causeways made it difficult. When Bill Northup and his friends from the Surf Garage in Narragansett finished trying to rescue people by boat along the waterfront, they went back to the center of town, where Police Chief Elmer Crossley told them to get over to the schoolhouse for a meeting. As soon as they arrived, he swore them in with fifteen other young men from town as deputies. He knew the local boys knew who lived in Narragansett and who didn't, so he authorized them to shoo away gawkers and help keep strangers, especially looters, out of town. Onlookers who appeared with their cameras and lunch boxes threatened to make a sideshow out of a local tragedy and were not welcome. There were reports of corpses being turned in at the morgues with their fingers cut off by looters who had found the bodies first and made off with their rings and jewelry.

Aclon Coggeshall went over to the Dunes Club, what was left of it, to help with the cleanup the following day and learned that Mrs. John Norris, who had been reluctant to leave the club the prior day for lunch, and her son had drowned. Her body had just been found under a roof that had blown into the pond where her car had flipped over when the tidal surge hit Narragansett.

Townspeople with summer and weekend homes grew anxious to know the extent of the damage to their property and playgrounds. A woman from Providence who went to look at her family's Sakonnet house found it moved fifty feet back from its foundation and the furnishings, most of them destroyed by wind and water, strewn about the yard. Standing alongside her neighbors, she stood and cried at the heaps of mud, fish, and lumber where their homes had once stood. The families who had been there told her again and again about the day of the hurricane. It was as though the re-telling would help them accept what had happened. They described soaking wet men emerging from waterfront pastures, filing up swamp roads, looking for clothes and food and places to rest. Their accounts of survivors washing up from Sakonnet Point, some on boats, some on rooftops, clinging to anything they could find to stay afloat when the wind and tidal wave converged, were nearly mythical. By the end of the day, listeners could recite the events as if they'd witnessed them for themselves.

Before the storm, Sakonnet, the flourishing little village of fishermen and shore restaurants that catered to steamers from Providence that brought people down for a shore lunch, had twenty-three buildings on the waterfront. Of them, only one lone support post was left standing when the sun rose the morning after the hurricane. One returning resident wrote in her diary that night, "We are all heartbroken. We did love our house and had worked so hard to make it perfect." She was one of the lucky ones. Her house had been merely damaged. Daylight streamed in where the roof was missing, but it was still standing.[22]

❋ ❋ ❋

It would be two weeks before downtown Providence was opened to traffic and normal business life resumed. The *Providence Bulletin* published a story that covered the effects of the storm on local businesses, including the news that most beauty parlors were still closed a week after the storm. WOMEN'S FACES REVERTING TO STATUS ORIGINALLY DESIGNED BY NATURE read the headline in that somewhat arch, smarty tone that seemed to distinguish comments on women's topics at the time. Cigarette ads that admonished, "Don't let your nerves get tired, upset" to promote smoking seemed to have a special resonance in the wake of the storm. The bronze plaque that marked the height the water had risen in a hurricane in 1815 was now a foot and a half below the most recent high-water mark.

David Patten had arranged with the publisher of the *Boston Post* to print the *Providence Bulletin* from the *Post*'s Boston offices until the basement of the *Bulletin*'s plant in Providence could be pumped out and made operative again. He and twenty-five staffers went by convoy to Boston, where Patten lived in the Statler Hotel for the next ten days, chronicling the disaster fifty miles away.

The Plum Beach lighthouse was badly damaged during the hurricane, but keepers Edwin Babcock and Johnny Ganze survived. The squat little lighthouse lost its railings in the storm and the basement filled with water while Babcock and Ganze survived above, lashed together to the lantern. Two days later they were rescued by two teenage boys who jumped in a rowboat they found ashore and rowed out to look around the lighthouse. Ganze and Babcock didn't need to be told how lucky they were. When they looked south toward the mouth of Narragansett Bay toward Whale Rock lighthouse, always in sight before the hurricane, there was nothing there. Its lighthouse keeper was never found. Ganze would move on to other lighthouses when the Plum Beach light was decommissioned the following year, but Babcock had seen enough.

❊ ❊ ❊

In Jamestown, the last of the bodies of the seven children who had drowned on Norm Caswell's school bus washed up more than two weeks later. A baby ring on the little girl's finger provided positive identification. She was first spotted when her skirt floated into sight on the bay, a speck of red on the water.[23]

❊ ❊ ❊

Though author Van Wyck Mason's journey from Nantucket to New Bedford with the manuscript of his new novel on his lap was tumultuous and had made him seasick, the coastal islands, Nantucket and Martha's Vineyard, suffered less than mainland waterfront areas. They were just far enough east of the hurricane's eye to be beyond its worst wrath, and the driving water could move around the islands, except where it found small inland waterways open to the sea, as were the narrow channels on the Vineyard's southwest end, facing the hurricane.

A group of three owners of Martha's Vineyard property set off jauntily by car from New York City to the Vineyard town of Chilmark to see what had happened to the
Barn House. This pre-Revolutionary farmhouse on South
Road was owned by Chilmark Associates, the town's largest nonresident property owners' cooperative. During summers its members slept in the old house on the property and
in remodeled chicken coops. They partied and ate dinner
in a large old barn that was the place's namesake. They also
owned a section of the Vineyard's South Beach, where they
swam and played through simple summers that satisfied the
yen of sophisticated New Yorkers to get back to nature and
the basics. It was a stylish notion of respite and relaxation
for many wealthy persons at the time. Simplicity, whimsy,
and play were luxuries to them.

Houston Kenyon, a patent attorney, made a report of
their trip. His account began like the log for a lark, wryly
characterizing his wife's uncle, a judge, who went along
on the trip as "custodian of the Bottle of Whiskey" because
he produced a flask of Armagnac brought back from a trip
to France. Apparently no outing or experience, even as dire
as hurricane damage inspection, was begun or reported
upon without a sense of irreverence and fun. But as their
journey progressed from New York City into Connecticut, where Kenyon reported that the scenic towns of
Guilford and Madison looked like "community woodpiles,"
signs of what they might find at the end of the day when
they reached Martha's Vineyard were ominous. In fact,
their property, Barn House, was high enough that it wasn't
damaged, but when the committee moved on to Menemsha,

Kenyon's jaunty tone changed. "Here was stark tragedy," he wrote.

The hurricane had ripped itself a new course through the landscape. Menemsha Basin was an interior pond that could not accommodate the twenty-five-foot-high waves and tons of water that had surged over Stonewall Beach on the south and swept everything in their path, including much of Chilmark's fishing harbor, into the Vineyard Sound on the north. The quaint little harbor dating back to the 1600s, with twelve buildings, most of them fishermen's shacks neatly lined up in picture postcard precision alongside small docks and moorings, was blown and washed away entirely except for one surviving structure, Carl Reed's Store. The tide was eight feet higher than any recorded in Chilmark's 244-year history.

Kenyon and his traveling party stood dumbly looking at the changes. The former sand spit was wiped clean of its docks and wasn't even a sand spit anymore. It had been torn from the mainland and was now an island.[24]

Closer to Stonewall Beach and the Atlantic on Stonewall Pond was the Benedict Thielen house, which had been completed three months earlier on blocks of concrete and creosoted piles. At the end of the hurricane, the blocks and piles, tilted 20 degrees away from the sea from where the wind and water had come, were all that remained. The house had been hurled well above the waterline near Stonewall Bridge. The Thielens, in residence the day of the hurricane, survived, but their West Indian cook, Mrs. Josephine Clark, drowned in a rushing wall of water that overtook them all as they were fleeing the house for higher ground. Josephine could not swim.

✽ ✽ ✽

At daybreak the morning after the storm, the Moore family on Barn Island spotted a bureau amid the wreckage that had washed ashore with them. Catherine recognized it from their Napatree house. The men dismantled the mirror atop it, and fifteen-year-old Geoffrey flashed signals in the bright sunlight. At first the gesture seemed idle, but a fishing boat offshore from Avondale saw the bright flash and came toward them. Wet, dirty, ragged, and covered with bits of hay, the Moores looked like a band of refugees as they ran out to meet it. Only eight-year-old Cathy seemed unhumbled by their experience. The fishing boat smelled bad, she said, and she refused to board it until a whack on the fanny from her father changed her mind. Safely onboard at last, Catherine broke down and clutched the girls to her, burying her face in their matted, wild hair. Jeff draped his arm around his son Geoff's shoulder and sagged with relief. May allowed herself a drink of whiskey offered by the crew, and was glad to get it. The crew gave the women their windbreakers, too. Everyone squeezed into the cabin, where the heat from the boat's engine began to warm them.

In the small world of coastal Rhode Island, Jeff Moore's brother Cy had a house in Avondale, so the boat captain knew where to take the family. When Cy saw who was on board, he ran to meet his brother, and he and Jeff Moore clung to each other and sobbed. During the next hour, the Moores learned about the scale of the storm and the devastation that had visited Misquamicut and Watch Hill.

The household helper, Nancy Liquori, was just fifteen years old and anxious to get back to her family. All phone lines were out, so the doctor who had been called to attend the Moores and Jim Nestor drove her home. The crowd outside her house was there to comfort her family, who had heard that morning on the street from a neighbor that the Geoffrey Moore family and staff had perished in the hurricane. Her father had started out to the Westerly High School, where the dead were taken, to look for her body. Nancy's family was overjoyed when she climbed out of the car, comically dressed in a long, green maid's uniform that the Cy Moore family had given her. She and the Moores soon learned that they were the lucky ones. Forty-two people had been in cottages on Fort Road on Napatree Point and all of them had been washed away. Fifteen had drowned.

The Geoffrey Moore family took a somewhat stoic approach in the aftermath of the hurricane. Catherine and Geoffrey Moore took the family back down to Napatree Point five days after the hurricane, as soon as the area was reopened. Even after their experience with the savagery of the storm, they were stunned when they saw the point. All of the thirty-nine houses that were standing on the morning of the hurricane had been washed away. To the amazement of everyone, there were almost no signs of the homes' seawalls or foundations. There were few piles of splintered wood and debris. The docks, the piers, the yacht clubs, the houses, the cars, and the boats were simply gone. Only the ruin of Fort Mansfield at the end of the road remained. It was as if all the others had never been there, as though the world had been made anew and was waiting to be populated for the first time.

The Moore children were gently prodded by their parents to go swimming. It seemed important to reestablish a friendly relationship with the sea. Their mother was most upset that all the family photos, moved into the Napatree house that summer, were ruined. Children playing in the sand nearby recovered some of Catherine's wedding silver that bore the family initials. They were mindful of the tragedy in the Butler house next door. Jim Nestor's aunt, Anne Nestor, the cook, and the laundress were all lost. The Moore family members listened to the stories of death and escape with sober expressions and lowered gazes. There was little formal grief counseling in those days, no expressed concerns for damaged psyches and barely suppressed traumas. Survivors turned away and moved on. The children looked to Catherine, who, it was apparent by then, was a pillar of emotional strength. They knew they would never forget their ordeal, and in their judgment the best thing to do was to get on with life. Catherine Moore seldom talked about the experience again with her children, though she wrote a detailed account of it for her brother. In closing, she wrote, "I sometimes feel that we have had a preview of the end of the world."[25]

Cathy missed the parrot that had been lost in the storm. She read in the paper that a fisherman in Stonington described finding one that sounded a lot like her Polly, but her parents said it couldn't be. It was their one assertion about the whole ordeal that she regarded with suspicion.

Local newspapers ran features on many of the survivors until some felt like celebrities. Mildred Larkham of Providence, who was the last to escape from Charlestown, was interviewed and photographed in her bedroom, which reporters described in detail down to the color (blue) of the cover on the bed in which she was recuperating. Her story of her family home being washed out from underneath her, taking her mother and best friend with it while she and her Scottie dog managed to float to safety on a board and a mattress, appeared in several papers. Though in shock and under a nurse's care, Mildred, nineteen, managed to talk to reporters: "Everyone of my family has thought for me all my life. I had no one but myself now. I just wouldn't think of anything more than clutching what I could, hanging on. I can't swim."[26] She attributed her survival to the winter coat she wrapped herself in before leaving the house. Many others had died of exposure.

For some, the end of the ordeal dragged on. Not knowing the fate of the missing seemed harder than knowing the worst. "Fort Roader" Paul Johnson Moore, who had returned to Schenectady, New York, with his wife and son while his seventy-year-old stepmother and sister stayed behind in their house on Napatree Point, experienced rain and strong winds in Schenectady, but Paul did not become alarmed until the next morning when his stepbrother phoned to say he had heard a newspaper reporter from Providence on his shortwave radio say that Fort Road was wiped out. Paul started out for Westerly the next morning, as did his father from New York. A friend accompanied him, and they discovered, much as the Chilmark Associates had, that signs of the hurricane became evident as they approached the coastline. In New Haven every tree seemed to be down. Each successive town toward the east had been harder hit. At Saybrook, Connecticut, four miles from Long Island Sound, a cabin cruiser blocked their lane in the Post Road. New London was almost impenetrable. Traffic moved at a snail's pace and was rerouted north of the city. When they arrived in Watch Hill, Paul's stepmother's body had been found, but his sister was missing. He was told that Fort Road was "all gone." Assisted by the Red Cross, local police, and volunteers, Jeff Moore (no relation to Paul) among them, Paul combed the swamps and wreckage looking for Havila. They stayed in Westerly with old acquaintances who could offer them a couch or daybed. Their hosts guided them to their rooms with lanterns and they sat at night talking by candlelight so long as the power was out. He heard from Kate Nestor that her nephew, who had sought safety during the hurricane with the Geoffrey Moore family, had tried to hurry her sister and the other women out of the house before the waves swept them to their deaths. "Hurry, Aunt Anne!" Jim had rushed her, but she had told him not to hurry her while she packed her handbag. Anne's body was found clutching her handbag. Her sister Kate broke down telling her story. Amid so much grief and his own quest, it was difficult to keep up morale. Paul looked on as Helen Joy Lee, now using crutches, was released from Westerly Hospital. He thought of Havila, whom he and his brother and father had often carried down into the ocean, where she could float and enjoy the physical freedom her handicap prevented on land. Everyone, even those who had suffered considerably, seemed to be moving on from the tragedy, but Paul and his father continued to search. A week after the hurricane, Paul decided to drive back to Schenectady for a few days. Rested, determined, and armed with a geodetic survey chart of Little Narragansett Bay, he returned to Westerly two days later, September 30, to continue the search. It was October 2, eleven days after the storm, when Havila's body was recovered from under a five-foot pile of wreckage in a cove opposite Woody Island, a place where Paul had stopped searching and turned back from a week earlier.[27]

Some survivors experienced a giddiness, a manic glad-to-be-alive mood once the worst was over, but soon the scale of the work ahead and the continuing effects of the hurricane—chiefly flooding—dampened such spirits. Swollen with runoff from the rain the hurricane had spilled as it collapsed inland, the coastal rivers (the Thames, Connecticut, Housatonic, and Merrimack) crested with floodwaters, spreading and continuing the catastrophe well into Friday, September 23. Bridges, dams, highways, and mills washed away.

Sandbags and work crews were routine parts of river-front life and easy to marshal, but in Hartford the Connecticut River was rising more than an inch per hour and townspeople feared that the dikes would not hold. As Hartford, seat of the American Red Cross headquarters, was preparing to help evacuees from the south, city engineers were grappling with how to protect the city itself from the continually rising waters. A triple row of sandbags was completed to form a slender buttress by 9:00 P.M., but by 11:00 the water was seeping through. Towns as far up the Connecticut as

Springfield, Massachusetts, evacuated residents. They were told to prepare for a crest of thirty-four and a half feet. The river ran right through the center of town. Fearful of the rising water, two hundred inmates rioted in the Hampden City jail in Springfield and had to be evacuated, adding to the mayhem. Townspeople in all the Connecticut River valley towns held their breath. Civic leaders prepared to dynamite dikes gradually in an effort to prevent the uncontrollable flood that would result if the dikes broke suddenly under pressure. The Connecticut River kept them guessing until 10:00 P.M. on Friday, when it stopped rising and began to recede.

From Long Island to Peterborough, New Hampshire, residents mourned the damage that the hurricane had done to New England's trees and forests. The rainy days that preceded the hurricane had left the soil loose and spongy and the grandest of trees vulnerable to the high winds. By one estimate, 275 million trees, some of them the pride of their New England towns, were down.[28] The Forest Service estimated that the timber from fallen trees was enough to build 200,000 five-room houses.[29] Half of the canopy of elms and locusts that lined the main street of East Hampton were felled by the hurricane. The last of the old forest between Water Mill and Southampton, Long Island, was totally blown down. On the Connecticut coast, travelers north began to see the real extent of the damage that Houston Kenyon on his trip to Martha's Vineyard had called "stark tragedy." In New Haven alone, five thousand trees that had lined the city's streets were destroyed. A sixth of the total were gone, and the town's tree superintendent predicted that New Haven would not look the same as it had before the hurricane for anywhere between twenty and forty years.[30]

As the storm moved inland, the winds had dropped, but the countryside was more vulnerable than the relatively hardened coastline. Sixteen thousand trees were uprooted in Springfield, Massachusetts, alone. Twenty-five hundred fell in Queens, New York. In Providence, Goddard Park, esteemed for its bosky, sprawling acreage, lost twenty-five thousand trees and was declared "ruined" in the newspapers.

The direction of treefall concerned meteorologists, who trusted it to be more accurate in charting the actual course of the hurricane and its wind changes than some of the instrument readings of the time. They rushed to study the carnage before the debris was hauled away. Some fallen trees were taken to sawmills and lumberyards, others were hauled to float on the lakes and ponds of New England where communities and mill yard operators hoped to preserve them. In Brookline, Massachusetts, the Lawrence farm lost two hundred trees. The owner set up a sawmill to salvage building lumber, and the rest was stacked in woodpiles to burn in stoves and fireplaces. The supply would last until 1980, when her grandson burned the last bundle. Residents of New England still often boast of houses and cottages built in part with lumber salvaged from the Great Hurricane of 1938.

Those trees left standing were a sobering reminder of what they had suffered. They were burned by the brine of the salty sea spray that had been swept forty miles inland from the ocean and made towns as far north as Worcester,

Massachusetts, look like they'd suffered a severe frost. It was disorienting. The brown and withered leaves looked more like December than September. The putrid smells of decomposing foliage, wood, and often unidentifiable and worrisome animal decay added a sense of the surreal.

The ecosystem throughout the Northeast was affected because sunlight could now reach the forest floor through the shattered tree canopy. The "windthrow," as botanists call the wind's ability to move soil and scatter seeds, also had an effect. The disturbance virtually eliminated the mature white pines that had been sown since the settlers first came to New Hampshire.[31] The bird life seemed to change, too. The brightly colored orioles that made big pocket nests high in the elm trees in Barrington, Rhode Island, didn't return. With most of the trees gone, they had no place to nest. Other, foreign species unknown to the local residents flew in to nest, pushed into the area by the hurricane winds. A yellow-billed tropic bird was picked up dead in Woodstock, Vermont, the first record of such a species that far north. A Cory's shearwater, common in the Carolinas, made its first appearance in New England, in Springfield, Massachusetts. It was assumed that the birds had been caught by the high winds and whirled into the hurricane's center where, supported on continually rising air, they traveled far from their native homes.[32]

Changes in human will were just as pivotal. The wealthy had already tightened their belts throughout the Depression. Some retrenched by selling off their summer homes on the shore or at least scaling down. Guest and chauffeur houses were rented for extra income or occupied as separate homes

. by extended family members. Farmlands on large estates were parceled out and sold.

The hurricane dealt the final blow to many who had held on through the Depression. When the hurricane washed out Mrs. Sharpe's rose gardens, once tended by Italian workers, at the end of Elm Lane in Barrington, Rhode Island, and blew away the wicker furniture she had loved to sit in looking out to sea, she lost heart. She and her husband, a furniture manufacturer from North Kingston, Rhode Island, decided not to restore their demolished summerhouse and gardens. The landscape was different now. The little natural trail that ran down to the sea at Nayatt Point and was such a delight had washed away entirely. The Sharpes decided to sell off parts of the land and subdivide the rest for development. It was the end of an era.

News of the disaster unfolded slowly, with the newspaper printing plants disabled and phone service out, but it began to reach the public the following day. HURRICANE KILLS AT LEAST 125 IN STATE, 29 DEAD, 52 MISSING IN WESTERLY, LOSS PUT IN MILLIONS, blared the *Providence Evening Bulletin.* A day later the count for Rhode Island had risen to 226 dead, 82 unreported, in the Rhode Island area with THE TOLL RISING declared the *Providence Journal,* now printed by the *Woonsocket Call* printing plant. By Sunday the twenty-fifth, the number of dead had risen to 250. The local papers told one sad story of death and drowning after another. There were tales of heroics like that of the Red Cross lifeguard in Weekapaug, Rhode Island, who swam across a forty-foot canal tethered to ten men by ropes onshore to rescue five stranded people.

And there were terrible, almost unthinkable, stories of family tragedies, like that of a young mother in Westerly who hung onto her four-year-old daughter by her dress until the skirt tore and the waves took the child out to sea.

* * *

From Boston, the *Providence Bulletin* continued to report on the Massachusetts primary and on the false lull from Europe, where on September 29, France and Britain allowed Hitler to annex Czechoslovakia and believed the threat of war had subsided. The *Bulletin* reported the events in a special edition called the "Peace Issue."

When the full impact of the storm was reported in Washington, President Roosevelt dispatched Harry Hopkins, the Works Progress Administration chief, to visit the area as his representative on September 26. Even five days after the fact, Hopkins found the disaster and destruction daunting. The devastation, he believed, warranted lifting the restrictions on WPA spending that had been previously in effect. He withdrew all hiring quotas and offered work to any able-bodied man at two to three times the previous WPA wages.

New England tried to dig itself out without power, passable roads, water, or phones. It took two hundred men until September 29 simply to open the roads and main streets to traffic in Newport. Most of the grand mansions were inland, protected by high ground, but when the ocean crashed over the seawall, the beaches were redrawn.

Power was restored to Providence one week after the hurricane, but downtown was closed to business and traffic for another two weeks. The funeral parlors were filled to capacity. Gillogly's in Westerly had sixty-six corpses. Refugees filled the armories, fire stations, and town and city buildings. The public was instructed to boil water and rationed to ten gallons of water per person per day. Health clinics ran out of typhoid vaccines. With roads closed due to the number of downed trees, mail was delivered by planes, the public's first glimpse of the airmail of the future. No newcomer to tragedy, James L. Feiser, chairman of the Red Cross, surveyed the situation and remarked publicly, "I have never seen a hurricane more complete in its devastation." He said he could not recall another instance of a whole community being struck so unawares. It would be several weeks before the lists of casualties were added up and the overall scale of devastation began to come into focus. Seven hundred people had died and 63,000 were left homeless. Nine thousand homes, cottages, and buildings were totally destroyed, and another 15,000 were damaged. More than five hundred thousand were without electricity.

In certain pockets of New England the damage was long-term. Depression-hobbled economies would take a decade to rebuild roads in certain areas. Three-quarters of the bluff in Watch Hill, Rhode Island, that had once been a central meeting place for American Indians was washed away forever. Fort Road on Napatree Point was never rebuilt. Some struggling textile mills in New England's river towns never reopened; the hurricane put an end to their tenuous operations. Others rebounded economically during the upcoming war effort when they became factories for guns and uniforms, but the good times were mostly temporary.

Fishing fleets and maritime communities, some that had begun within a decade of the Pilgrims' landing, were nearly wiped out. A total of 2,605 vessels were destroyed and 3,369 were reported damaged. Where 100 commercial fishing boats and 650 fishermen had fished the waters between New London and Point Judith before the hurricane, only three boats remained.[33] On Long Island, 200 fishermen and their families were left homeless when the Montauk fishing village was wiped out. Over 12,000 persons declared themselves dependent on the Red Cross in nearby Riverhead.

✳ ✳ ✳

The mild, beautiful weather that followed the day after the hurricane felt almost like a mockery of what New England had been through. How could there be such peace and loveliness in the wake of the monster that had just passed? Such glorious blue skies overhead while people worked amid wreckage and buried their dead? A new day dawned in the heavens, but those who read the papers or lived in the hurricane's path knew what the Great Hurricane of 1938 had taken with it. Gone were the seaside roller coasters and carousels, the shore dinner restaurants and the clubs and dance pavilions where only weeks before many had danced under starlight. Nearly every small coastal New England town had changed profile when church spires were toppled from Sag Harbor, Long Island to Keene, New Hampshire. For more than a century the steeples had dominated the village views and welcomed the whalers. Their destruction was often the least of the real damage, but they symbolized a greater loss, as if their toppling was proof of a brush with some apocalyptic power. The cleanup effort stretched ahead endlessly.

It was the brainy and bookish meteorologist of Bridge-hampton, Long Island, Ernest Clowes, who took it upon himself to challenge the Weather Bureau's failure to report the coming of the hurricane. He wrote to C. L. Mitchell, head of the Forecast Division of the U.S. Weather Bureau in Washington. What was the reason, he asked Mitchell, "why we folks out here received no adequate warnings before the hurricane was actually upon us." He was moved to begin writing a book about the hurricane on Long Island, and the day following the hurricane he wrote to the editor of the *New York Times*. "I wish that public criticism could be warmed up against the tragic insufficiency of warning of the recent hurricane that brought death to many persons on this island." He railed that "whole gale" warnings, such as happen half a dozen times any winter, were all the public received. He blamed Washington. Mitchell replied to the challenges in a lengthy letter to Charles Brooks, head of the Blue Hill Observatory in Milton, Massachusetts, who joined Clowes in his research and questioning of the bureau. (Perhaps Mitchell considered Brooks, in his professional capacity at the prestigious Blue Hill, more worthy of his written reply.) His response was thin. He lamented the rudimentary nature of weather predictions at the time and went so far as to single out shoddy cloud observations in Nantucket, a good hundred miles east of the hurricane's path. He blamed the quality of observation in New England and New York, especially from the Nantucket South Shoals Lightship station.

"Nantucket is a key station for us in such cases, and the
cloud observations there have been so unsatisfactory." He
said that he had requested the successor to the current observer be sent to either Washington or the Blue Hill Observatory "for some real instruction in cloud observing." The
compliment to the Blue Hill Observatory did not pacify
Brooks. "My chief criticism relates to the Bureau's forecast
intended for the general public," Brooks wrote back, adding, "There was no mention of wind." He closed his letter
by suggesting that the bureau make arrangements with the
readers of all tide heights along the coast to report devia-
tions in sea level. In the end, the old-timers who watched
and timed the roller waves and swells had been more reliable. Brooks shared Mitchell's response with Ernest Clowes,
who commented, "I thought Mitchell's letter to you was
pretty bad. From it, it would seem everyone was to blame
from God to the unfortunate field observers." He wished
Mitchell would have simply said that the forecast was in-
adequate and too late.

Instead, Mitchell stubbornly asserted, "I believe, and
most others at the Central Office apparently share my belief, that this office handled the storm situation at least fairly
well under the circumstances."

❊ ❊ ❊

The Great Hurricane of 1938 became history quickly. It
never was big news outside the East Coast region. Without
television news, the rest of the country hardly knew it happened. And eventually it would begin to recede even in the
Eastern consciousness as its survivors passed on.

Firsthand recollections of the Great Hurricane of 1938 survive only in the dogged memory of a few remaining survivors. For some, the indelibly intense experiences have outlived in memory many of life's other main events and vicissitudes. Eighty and ninety-year-olds who lived through the hurricane often can barely remember the names of children or the years of their births anymore. Each year time wipes their memories a bit cleaner. But the events on September 21, 1938, have stayed remarkably clear in memory. As following generations remember where they were when they heard that President Kennedy had been shot or of the attack on the World Trade Center towers on 9/11, so these aged survivors of GH38 preserve vivid accounts of their experiences during the worst storm in New England's history.

Occasionally, a tourist to Westerly, Watch Hill, or Narragansett wonders where the splendid old homes and historic neighborhoods that exist in certain shoreline pockets of New England, Maine, and Nantucket might have gone over the years. Seaside communities of a slowly reemerging prosperous class at the end of the Depression were in some cases completely washed away by the hurricane. Some had been the cornerstone of a quietly privileged life that had been burgeoning in coastal New England's summer centers, chief among them Westerly and Watch Hill in Rhode Island and the Hamptons in New York. Some towns, like Westerly, never quite regained the cachet of their pre-1938 selves. Watch Hill, though seriously damaged, rebounded. In Charlestown, Rhode Island, 160 of its 200 houses, including the Rhode Island Yacht Club, were entirely obliterated, as was the nearby fishing community of Gallilee.

❊ ❊ ❊

GH38 was more than just another major storm. Though they were largely forgotten by 1938, there had been many hurricanes in New England before. Some had been considered merely tropical storms, typical for the fall season. The hurricane of 1815 may have come closest to approximating the strength of the Great Hurricane of 1938, but the coastline was far less populated then, and in 1815 there were fewer weather observers or news organizations to record and broadcast its damage and effects. As Paul Moore noted in 1938, in 1815 there was only one cottage on Napatree Point, where 39 stood in 1938. On September 8, 1869, a lesser hurricane covered a smaller area of southern New England, but it struck further north and caused extensive damage in Boston, Massachusetts, and Portland, Maine.[34] Five other tropical cyclones followed in the twentieth century before GH38, but none was as deadly or as memorable.

GH38 hit the most densely populated area in the richest country in the world and in a matter of four hours humbled it. Newspaperman and author Everett S. Allen tallied in his book, *A Wind to Shake the World* (Little, Brown, 1976): "Seven hundred and eight suffered injuries; 4,500 homes, summer cottages, and farm buildings were destroyed; 15,139 homes, summer cottages, and farm buildings were damaged; 2,605 boats were lost and 3,369 were damaged. A total of 19,608 families applied for emergency help or assistance in rehabilitating themselves.

"Twenty-six thousand automobiles were smashed; 275,000,000 trees were broken off or uprooted, amounting to 2.6 billion board feet of timber downed, and nearly 20,000 miles of electric power and telephone lines were blown or knocked down. A total of 1,675 head of livestock and between 500,000 and 750,000 chickens were killed. Railroad service between New York and Boston was interrupted for seven to fourteen days while 10,000 men filled 1,000 washouts, replaced nearly 100 bridges and removed thousands of obstructions from the tracks, including a number of houses and 30 boats. More than a half-million telephones were silenced, isolating 240 communities.

"The storm destroyed $2,610,000 worth of fishing boats, equipment, docks, and shore plants . . ."

In retrospect, what distinguished the GH38 from other storms at other times and places was the heightened sense of hurt and surprise—almost of unfairness—that accompanied it. The storm struck a vulnerable part of the country when it was in a weakened economic state, and it came without warning, like a sneak punch. The national psyche was fragile. New England, with its great dependence on traditional manufacturing, was particularly susceptible to physical damage. With will and work and character, the region had persevered through the Depression. So it was a bit like watching a young American hero overcome the odds against him to succeed, only to be robbed and whipped without warning or reason by a bully twice his size. That is how it looks from the present, but there was little evidence of self-pity at the time. As Ernest Clowes wrote in the book he completed, *Hurricane of 1938 on Eastern Long Island* (Hampton Press, 1939), it was the "irrepressible American reaction of ironical and slightly hysterical gayety toward stunning loss" that characterized the spirit of the moment. The long-term effects on the economy, the mills, tourism, and the fishing industries would settle in later. As an American disaster, it was unrivaled at the time. GH38's loss of lives and property damage total exceeded San Francisco's earthquake and fire of 1906 and Chicago's fire of 1871.

It was also a unique disaster because the surprise generated by its sudden appearance guaranteed that the country would not be caught off guard again. Advances in weather-tracking and communications developed rapidly in its wake. The shortwave radio schedules tested by the New England Power system during GH38 would become a regular network in the months that followed.[35] Additional reporting and vigilant tracking by the U.S. Weather Bureau was in part a response to GH38. The following year, the bureau began making four daily forecasts instead of two.[36] By 1940, meteorologists were more reliably tracking storms. Storms today create damage, death, and havoc, but they are unable to surprise. In some ways, GH38 was the first and last of its kind as it disappeared into the mists of Canada.

In other ways, it was like the attack on the World Trade Center in September 2001. Of course, the hurricane was a natural rather than a human enemy that attacked. But both were on a scale that people simply did not think could happen, and the sense of hurt and violation, and to some degree wonder, would be long remembered. Though GH38 was quickly crowded off the front pages outside New England by the drums of war in Europe, it would never be forgotten as the time when the public in New England came to understand that large events, bad things beyond their making, could strike even on their doorstep.

Protectiveness figured more prominently into people's thinking after the hurricane. For reasons of finance and prudence, the thirty-nine homes on Napatree Point were not replaced. Even New Englanders who had the money to rebuild were wary of building so close to the water. It didn't seem like such a good idea. Homeowners insurance, rare in 1938 and only covering fire when it was in effect, would not catch on until after the war.

On September 24 a story entitled "Czechs Prepare for War" shared the front page of the *Providence Journal* with the latest news that the storm toll in Rhode Island had reached 240. By the twenty-seventh the situation had escalated to "Hitler Threatens War unless Czechs Yield Sudetenland." While hurricane adventures and more exact counts of the dead filled the inside pages, war news of Europe took back the front pages of even the local papers. Within several weeks the hurricane, though the recovery effort was far from over, had become old news. While one world was about to be changed by war, another had already been completely washed away on a Wednesday afternoon in September between two and six o'clock.

Notes

1. David Longshore, "Andrew, Hurricane," in *Encyclopedia of Hurricanes, Typhoons, and Cyclones* (New York: Checkmark Books, 2000), p. 10.

2. Perry and Shuttleworth, "In the Eye of the Hurricane by Mrs. Norvin Greene (Tot)," *The 1938 Hurricane as We Remember It* (Quogue Historical Society, East Patchogue, NY: Searle Graphics, 1998), p. 8.

3. Katharine Hepburn, "Hurricane," in *Me: Stories of My Life* (New York: Alfred A. Knopf, 1991), pp. 210–14.

4. Paul J. Moore, *The Search: An Account of the Fort Road Tragedy* (Westerly, RI: Sun Graphics, 1988).

5. Perry and Shuttleworth, "George E. Burghard," in *The 1938 Hurricane,* vol. 2, p. 20.

6. Ernest Clowes, *The Hurricane of 1938 on Eastern Long Island* (Bridgehampton, NY: Hampton Press, 1939).

7. Perry and Shuttleworth, "Arthur D. Raynor," in *The 1938 Hurricane,* vol. 2, p. 9.

8. Alice Lovejoy, "Waiting, 1938," the Klyberg Papers, Rhode Island Historical Society.

9. David R. Vallee and Michael Dion, *Southern New England Tropical Storms and Hurricanes* (National Weather Service), p. 128, and William Elliott Minsinger, *The 1938 Hurricane* (Blue Hill Observatory, 1988), p. 26.

10. Everett S. Allen, chapter 8, in *A Wind to Shake the World* (Boston: Little, Brown, 1976), pp. 142–53.

11. Hammond, "The Escape of Mr. and Mrs. Geoffrey Moore and Their Family," *Seaside Topics* 35 (November 1938): p. 5.

12. Hammond, "Mrs. Helen Joy Lee," *Seaside Topics* 35 (November 1938): p. 7.

13. "Lashed," the Klyberg Papers, Rhode Island Historical Society.

14. R. A. Scotti, *Sudden Sea* (New York: Little, Brown, 2003) p. 180.

15. Allen, "The Rescue of Pierrepoint Johnson Jr.," *A Wind to Shake the World*, p. 219.

16. Mike Stanton, "The Prosecutor, the Priest, and the Mob Boss," in *The Prince of Providence* (New York: Random House, 2003), p. 7.

17. *Providence Bulletin*, September 27, 1938.

18. Allen, *A Wind to Shake the World*, p. 197.

19. Joe McCarthy, *Hurricane!* (New York: American Heritage Press, 1969), p. 111.

20. Allen, *A Wind to Shake the World*, p. 112.

21. Longshore, *Encyclopedia of Hurricanes*, p. 154.

22. Diary of Mabel Bartlett Stokes, Rhode Island Historical Society.

23. Scotti, *Sudden Sea*, pp. 218–19.

24. Houston Kenyon Jr., "The Hurricane of 1938: Chilmark's Great Trauma," *Dukes County Intelligencer* (Edgartown, MA: Dukes County Historical Society, 1994), pp. 24–36.

25. Hammond, "Escape of Mr. and Mrs Geoffrey Moore," p. 7.

26. *Providence Bulletin*, Edith A. Nichols, "Mildred C. Larkham Last Person to Escape," September 27, 1938, p. 4.

27. Moore, *The Search*, p. 95.

28. Allen, *A Wind to Shake the World*, p. 349.

29. McCarthy, *Hurricane!* p. 138.

30. Allen, *A Wind to Shake the World*, p. 95.

31. William Holland Drury Jr., *Chance and Change* (Berkeley and Los Angeles: University of California Press, 1998), p. 101.

32. *The Auk: A Quarterly Journal of Ornithology*, American Ornithologists' Union 56, Fayetteville, Arkansas, 1939, pp. 176–79.

33. Allen, *A Wind to Shake the World*, p. 139.

34. James A. Grant, "Engineering Aspects of the New England Hurricane of 1938," *The Military Engineer* 31, no. 176 (March–April 1939): p. 80.

35. "Short Wave Radio," in *Contact*, Flood and Hurricane Issue, New England Power Association, Boston, vol. 19, no. 11 (November 1938): p. 24.

36. Donald Whitman, *A History of the United States Weather Bureau* (Donald Whitman, 1961), p. 136.

Acknowledgments

This book could not have been written without the help of others. My sincere thanks to Caroline Ellis and Suzanne Cavedon, who introduced me to the hurricane by sharing their own family tragedies, to my agent Todd Shuster at the Zachary Shuster Harmsworth Literary Agency for his unflinching support, to my editor Joan Bingham at Grove/Atlantic for her steadfast guidance and enthusiasm, to Lindsay Sagnette, also at Grove, for guiding this book to publication, and to my husband Dick Duncan for his enduring patience, generosity, and literary contribution.

I am extremely grateful to the dozens of hurricane survivors who shared their stories with me and for their patience with a reporter asking detailed questions about an event that had occurred sixty-five years ago as though it were only yesterday. I am indebted to Catherine Moore Driscoll, Lee Pierce, the late Aclon Coggeshall, Adams Nickerson, Emily Fowler, Jean Almgren, Anna Sisk, Richard

Hendrickson, Bill Northup, Jack Tobin, Milt Miller, Steven Dellapolla, Helen Bengtson Vorpahl, Frederick Williamson, Daphne Root, Patricia Driver Shuttleworth, Marilyn Fogel Schlossberg, Carlton Brownell, Prentice Lanphere, and Lindsay Green, Ceci Sartor, Sallye Stephenson, Weedy Block, and Charles Wright, who helped me make contact. There are others too numerous to list who went out of their way to help me reconstruct the human story of the Great Hurricane of 1938. David Michaelis lent me significant research material. Nat Philbrick involuntarily became my confessor. The aid and cooperation of the staff of the Rhode Island Historical Society, Richard Klyberg, Maurice Gibbs, Tammy Murray, and the residents of the Laurelmead Cooperative in Providence, Rhode Island, were most valuable to this work. Thank you to each and every one.

I must also thank my children, Jessie and Alex Duncan, who are patient with the dramas of a writing mother and vigilant at their job of keeping me from taking myself too seriously. I never failed to laugh when I retreated, somewhat self-victimized, to my study to work, as Alex called out behind me, ". . . and the wind blew harder and harder and harder."

Index